TOM SEYI

Wild Plants
of Maine

A USEFUL GUIDE

FOURTH EDITION

Printed in the United States of America

© 2023 Tom Seymour

All rights reserved. No part of this publication may be reproduced (except for reviews), stored in a retrieval system, or transmitted in any form by any means, electronic, mechanical, photocopying, recording or otherwise, without the written prior permission of the publisher and/or author.

Photos: 2018 © Tom Seymour

Seymour, Tom
Tom Seymour: Wild Plants of Maine:
A Useful Guide
p. 190
1. Nature : Plants - General. 2. Nature : Plants - Mushrooms.
3. Nature : Ecosystems & Habitats - Coastal Regions & Shorelines
I. Title.

ISBN: 978-1-0882-5290-1

Published by:
Mt. Waldo Publishing
Frankfort, Maine 04086
www.tomseymourmaine.com

First Just Write Books Edition 2010
Fourth Edition: First Mt. Waldo Publishing Edition 2023

Printed in the United States of America

Dedication

I dedicate this book to my parents and grandparents, who, instead of imposing artificial restraints upon my free time when a child, allowed me to roam freely through the woods and fields, investigating, inspecting and identifying every wild plant, animal, bird, fish and insect that came across my path.

These early woodland wanderings led to a lifelong love of nature and a fuller appreciation of the natural world around us, a love that culminated in the form of this book.

I also wish to thank my friend and publisher, Nancy E. Randolph, who has given me direction, support and love over these many years. Thank you, Nancy.

For many years, Tom Seymour lived in this small cabin in the woods in Waldo, Maine growing and foraging his food when he was not fishing or writing about our natural environment and other outdoor pursuits.

Tom has since moved to Frankfort, Maine, where he pastors a small church and lives quietly in a small town surrounded by his friends and parishioners. He continues to write, fish, forage and garden in his new home.

Content

Plant Names   v

Preface   ix

Introduction   I

Tools for collecting   3
Hazards   4
Plant Structure   5

Spring   7

Evening Primrose   7
Cattail Sprouts   10
Coltsfoot   12
Blunt-Leaved Dock   13
Dandelion   15
Fiddleheads (Ostrich Fern)   17
Orpine   19
Curled Dock   20
Japanese Knotweed   21
Stinging Nettles   23
Purple Trillium   26
Trout Lily   27
Jewelweed   29
Large-Leaved Aster   30
False Solomon's Seal   32
Wild Oats   33
Clintonia   34
Wintercress   36
Garlic Mustard   38
Common Blue Violet   40
Groundnuts   42
Partridgeberry   45
Wild Sarsaparilla   45

Summer   47

Wild Mint   47
Wild Horseradish   50
Dame's Rocket   52
Pickerelweed   54
Comfrey   55
Common Milkweed   57
Cattail   60
Common Plantain   63
Indian Cucumber   64
Valerian   65
Heal-All   67
Pineapple Weed   68
Queen Anne's Lace   69
Sweetfern   71
Daylilies   74
Oxeye Daisy   76
Pearley Everlasting   78
Tansy   79
Elderberry   81
Blueberries   84
Beaked Hazelnuts   85
Arrowhead   87
Purslane   88
Serviceberry   89
Galinsoga   91
Lady's Thumb   93
Skullcap   94
Peppergrass   95
Lamb's Quarters   96
Green Amaranth   99
Joe-Pye Weed   100
Jewelweed   101
Wild Parsnip   103
Soapwort   104
Staghorn Sumac   106
St. Johnswort   107

Maine's Seashore 109

Beach Pea 109
Sea Blite 111
Glasswort 112
Sea Rocket 114
Orache 115
Goosetongue 117
Northern Bay 119

Fall 123

Goldthread 123
Boneset 126
Canada Goldenrod 127
Wintergreen 128
White Pine 130
Eastern Hemlock 131
Beechnuts 133

Wild Mushrooms 137

Shaggy Mane Mushroom 138
Chanterelles 140
Black Trumpets 142
Coral Mushroom 145
Painted Bolete 147
Hen of the Woods 148
Chicken of the Woods 150
Puffballs 152
Chaga 154

Winter 157

Recipes 159

Pickled Pickerel 159
Blue Mussels 160
Stovies 161

Nettle Soup 161
Knotweed Chutney 162
Garlic Knotweed 162
Fiddlehead and Cheese
    Sauce Casserole 163
Fiddlehead Salad 163
Canned Fiddleheads 163
Nancy's Fiddleheads 164
Penny's Sauteed Fiddleheads 164
Wilted Dandelion Salad 165
India-style Dandelion 166
Simple Woods Scramble 167
Chanterelles 167
Coral Mushrooms 167
Blueberries 167
Elderberry Fritters 168
Milkweed Blossom Fritters 168
Northern Bay Nutlets 168
Trout Lily 169
Wild Mint 169
Elderberry Cordial 170
Elderberry Jelly 170
Dandelion Wine 171
Staghorn Sumac "Pink
    Lemonade" 171

Resources 172

Books by Tom Seymour 173

Index 175

Wild plant seminars 181

About the Author 181

Plant Names

Common Name	Botanical Name
Arrowhead	*Sagittaria latifolia*
Beach Pea	*Lathyrus japonicus*
Beechnut	*Fagus grandifolia*
Beaked Hazelnuts	*Corylus cornuta*
Black Trumpets	*Craterellus fallax*
Blueberries	*Vaccinium corymbosum*
Blunt-Leaved Dock	*Rumex obtusifolius*
Boneset	*Eupatorium perfoliatum*
Canada Goldenrod	*Solidago canadensis*
Cattail	*Typha latifolia*
Chaga	*Inonotus obliquus*
Chanterelles	*Cantharellus cibarius*
Chicken of the Woods	*Laetiporus sulphureus*
Clintonia	*Clintonia borealis*
Coltsfoot	*Tussilago farfara*
Comfrey	*Symphytum officinale*
Common Blue Violet	*Viola papilionacea*
Common Milkweed	*Asclepias syriaca*
Common Plantain	*Plantago major*
Coral Mushroom	*Clavaria*
Curled Dock	*Rumex crispus*
Dame's Rocket	*Hesperis matronalis*
Dandelion	*Taraxacum officinale*
Daylilies	*Hemerocallis fulva*
Eastern Hemlock	*Tsuga Canadensis*
Elderberry	*Sambucus canadensis*
Evening Primrose	*Oenothera biennis*
False Solomon's Seal	*Smilacina racemosa*
Fiddleheads	*Matteuccia strathiopteris*
Galinsoga	*Galinsoga ciliata*
Garlic Mustard	*Alliaria petiolata*
Glasswort	*Salicornia virginica*
Goldthread	*Coptis groenlandica*
Goosetongue	*Plantago juncoides*
Green Amaranth	*Amaranthus retroflexus*
Groundnuts	*Apios americana*
Heal-All	*Prunella vulgaris*

Hen of the Woods .... *Grifola frondosa*
Indian Cucumber.............. *Medeola virginiana*
Japanese Knotweed............*Polygonum cuspidatum*
Jewelweed......................*Impatiens capensis*
Joe-Pye Weed .... *Eupatorium maculatum*
Lady's Thumb................ *Polygonum persicaria*
Lamb's Quarters.............. *Chenopodium album*
Large-Leaved Aster.............. *Aster macrophyllus*
Northern Bay .... *Myrica pensylvanica*
Orache ....*Atriplex patula*
Orpine .... *Sedum purpureum*
Oxeye Daisy........ *Chrysanthemum leucanthemum*
Painted Bolete Mushroom .... *Boletinus pictus*
Partridgeberry................... *Mitchella repens*
Pearley Everlasting .... *Anaphalis margaritacea*
Peppergrass.................. *Lepidium campestre*
Pickerelweed................... *Pontederia cordata*
Pineapple Weed ....*Matricaria matricarioides*
Puffballs.......................*Calvatica species*
Purple Trillium................. *Trillium erectum*
Purslane ....*Portulaca oleracea*
Queen Anne's Lace................ *Daucus carota*
Sea Blite .... *Suaeda maritima*
Sea Rocket ....*Cakile edentula*
Serviceberry .... *Amelanchier laevis*
Shaggy Mane Mushroom .... *Coprinus comatus*
Skullcap .... *Scutellaria lateriflora*
Staghorn Sumac....................*Rhus typhina*
Soapwort.................... *Saponaria officinalis*
St. Johnswort .... *Hypericum perforatum*
Stinging Nettles .... *Urtica dioica*
Sweetfern ....*Comptonia perigrina*
Tansy .... *Tanacetum vulgare*
Trout Lily...............*Erythronium americanum*
Valerian .... *Valeriana officinalis*
White Pine .... *Pinus strobus*
Wild Horseradish ....*Armoracia rusticana*
Wild Mint .... *Mentha arvensis*
Wild Oats.................. *Smilacina racemosa*
Wild Parsnip.................. *Pastinaca sativa*
Wild Sarsaparilla .... *Aralia nudicaulis*
Wintercress....................*Barbarea vulgaris*
Wintergreen ....*Gaultheria procumbens*

Preface

This book was originally released by Just Write Books, of Topsham, Maine. Now, Nancy E. Randolph, publisher, has sought new challenges and to the regret of many, has left the publishing business. Nancy has kindly turned over publishing of my books to me. My new publishing house, Mt. Waldo Publishing, will continue to publish all the books originally produced by Just Write Books.

Will there be more books of this nature in the future? It seems likely, since not having a book to work on leaves an empty spot in my life.

Introduction

It hardly seems possible that thirteen years have passed since *Wild Plants of Maine* was first published. Even so, the book is now in its fourth edition and sometime in the future, a fifth edition should follow.

One reason for revising a book on wild plants is not that the plants change in any way, but rather, new plants and new uses for them continually come to light. Remember, though, that this a book on wild, useful plants of Maine, and some species, beloved as they may be south of here, cannot be included because they do not occur in Maine.

But Maine holds enough wonders of its own. Also, readers and participants in plant walks often shed new light on old plants. I would be remiss not to assemble these bits of information and add them to a new edition.

For now, though, *Wild Plants of Maine,* will begin its new life with a new publishing company, Mt. Waldo Publishing.

My thanks go out to all who have bought and read my book. It particularly pleases me when I meet someone with a dog-eared, dirt-stained, falling-apart copy. This tells me that this person has thoroughly delved into the subject of Maine's wild, useful plants, briars included. And, after all, that is my goal. Good reading, and I wish you all well.

After reading this, it immediately occurred to me that in so many cases, disaster might easily be averted if only people were familiar with wild edible plants. Surely, particularly in tropical areas of the world, sufficient wild foods exist so that no one ever need go hungry.

Here in America, many folks equate eating wild plants with tough, economic times. This especially rings true for older people, those who struggled through the end of the Great Depression. For them, dandelions, dock, cattails, fiddleheads and the rest represent something they would just as soon forget. And then there are those who consider wild plants as something less than good food. Interesting perhaps, but not the real thing. These same people happily purchase commercially-raised vegetables from stores, while at the same time eschewing the wild edibles growing in their very dooryard.

Hopefully, this book can help change all that. The plants covered here are certainly not the only useful, wild plants found in Maine. Rather, they are the plants that I personally deal with. As such, they represent a good cross-section of food types, from leafy greens to root crops, trail nibbles (meant to be eaten out of hand, raw) to flour substitutes.

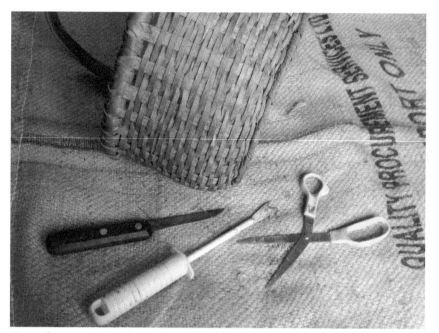

Every forager needs only simple tools such as a knife, a weeding tool and a regular pair of scissors while harvesting wild edibles and other useful plant.

During a lifetime of familiarity with wild edibles, I have come to regard wild foods as far superior to commercial products. Consider this. Wild plants are a pure food and grow just fine without any help from chemicals and pesticides. The soil where these plants grow is of their own choosing. This is truly a big deal and here's why.

When we plant a cultivated vegetable, we must go to lengths to ascertain that our soil is of the proper acidity for that species, that it contains the proper nutrients and that it is neither too dry nor too wet. Then we must consider location, which translates to the amount of sunlight or shade the plant receives each day. All these concerns add up to one, big balancing act—an act that few of us ever fully get right.

But wild plants select their own location. They simply do not thrive in unsuitable conditions. If an edible wild plant grows someplace it is because that location suits it. A simple thing, but good to know because different plants have different requirements.

For instance, wild evening primrose thrives in nutrient-depleted soil. As such, they are indicators of soil type. Conversely, stinging nettles absolutely require rich, nutrient-laden soil. Want to plant a garden? If nettles grow on your land, that ground is guaranteed to be rich, just right for all kinds of domestic vegetables.

A basket or canvas tote makes the best gathering container.

Herbs, on the other hand, pack the most punch when grown in poor soil. So let the wild evening primrose show you just where that thyme and oregano will grow to best advantage.

My love affair with wild edibles knows no bounds. Others may not care to immerse themselves to a similar extent, but nearly everyone can benefit from gleaning a passing acquaintance with the wild edible plants that grow all around us. At the least, it's a fascinating hobby. Taken further, it can help trim grocery bills while at the same time providing healthful, vitamin-packed food. What more could anyone ask?

Tools for collecting

Most plants require only hand-picking. A few, such as tubers and other root crops, must be dug. Usually, a hand trowel will suffice. Dandelions are best harvested with the help of a commercially-available dandelion digger. This somewhat resembles a screwdriver, only the blade, instead of being flat, is forked. This allows the harvester to insert the blade under the plant's crown and with a gentle twist, pop crown, leaves and a bit of root out of the ground in one, quick move.

As important as digging tools are the containers that we put our plants in as we harvest them. The big consideration here is to use something made of a material that breathes, a medium that allows air exchange. Never, ever, put plants in a plastic bag. This causes them to wilt and to sweat. In time, if left in the bag, the plant will become moldy.

I favor a basket made of brown ash. These, if well cared for, should last a lifetime. Alternately, I always have a few canvas tote bags stashed in the trunk of my car. These allow the plants to breathe and also help to keep them cool and fresh. Never leave a container filled with wild plants in direct sunlight.

Sometimes, if I know I am going to harvest a sizeable quantity of plants, perhaps for the freezer, I carry an ice chest. But instead of ice, which can wet the plants and cause nearly as much damage as if they were placed in a plastic bag, I use sealed containers. The simplest thing here is just to fill a few plastic jugs with water and keep them in the freezer. When needed, pop them in the ice chest.

Hazards

Any activity that takes us out-of-doors in the State of Maine has the potential to expose us to some unpleasant circumstances. Poison ivy and wild clematis, two toxic plants that cause itchy, sometimes painful rashes, exist throughout the state. Learn to identify these plants and, thus, avoid them.

And then we have insects. Maine humorists often include black fly jokes in their repertoire. These little monsters inject something like novocaine into their victim's flesh prior to biting. Most of the time, we don't even realize that a half-dozen black flies are biting us and lapping up our blood.

Mosquitoes, always a nuisance, now represent a bigger threat than in years past. Some nasty viruses are spread via infected mosquitoes. And ticks, once just somewhat distasteful little pests, now carry Lyme disease and other debilitating diseases.

So what's the answer? Simply this. Protect yourself from biting insects and toxic plants by wearing long-sleeved shirts and pants. The more exposed skin, the greater the risk of being bitten by a potentially diseased insect. Also, a liberal application of insect repellent probably helps as much as anything. Some people eschew chemical repellents, in favor of natural formulas. In my experience, the natural stuff, if it works at all, has a limited period of effectiveness. Accordingly, I prefer repellents containing DEET.

As soon as I come in from outdoors, I wash the repellent off and thus far, have noticed no ill effects. It's up to the individual to choose, but my vote goes to the "better safe than sorry" side.

However, reports of another, non-DEET repellent, picaridin, sold as a DEET alternative, sounds promising. Both the World Health Organization and Centers for Disease Control endorse picaridin as an effective repellent and safe alternative to DEET. I'm told that this product performs as well as DEET containing repellents, but without any of the drawbacks. It sounds like a true panacea, one whose advent was a long time coming.

A portion of this book is devoted to medicinal wild plants. As with any endeavor, prudence and good judgment are essential. Never use any wild plant as medicine without first consulting a health-care professional. In some cases, life-threatening drug interactions can occur. So remember, just because these are innocent-looking plants, don't automatically think that they are ineffective or totally benign. The constituents in wild plants, although natural as opposed to processed, are just as potent as anything else we may take as medicine.

A physician friend who has an interest in wild plants recommended consulting www.naturaldatabase.com. It is a subscription site and serves as an online physician's desk reference. It contains drug interaction warnings. Persons who take a serious interest in wild plants as medicine should consider investigating this site. Or, perhaps, your personal physician has access to this and can consult it on your behalf.

The small number of medicinal plants covered here are those that I use myself. Each year, I harvest and process my "medicine plants." This is necessary because the shelf life on any plant material seldom lasts much more than one year. Anyway, these plants work for me and that's the long and short of it. Learn about them, but ask your doctor before taking any plant medicine.

The recipes included here are just the ways that I like to prepare my plants. Feel free to improvise, add and subtract. Make up your own recipes. That's part of the fun of being a forager.

Plant Structure

Throughout the book, you will see that plants are described according to their physical attributes. Some terms may seem foreign at first, but upon reading a description and looking at the actual plant, you will see that they really are helpful and not at all difficult to decipher. Let me cite an example.

A plant may be described as having alternate, finely toothed leaves. This just means that the leaves appear alternately on the stipe or stem, as opposed to directly opposite each other. Lots of times, these pairs make a half-twist from bottom to top. This allows the plant to gather the maximum amount of sunlight and thus produce chlorophyll.

Other descriptions will describe a leaf's shape. This may be lance-shaped (long and slender), ovate (egg-shaped) or in a whorl (numbers of leaves radiating from a central point). In only a short time, you will come to rely upon these descriptions to help in proper identification of new plants. In fact, never, ever, eat or otherwise ingest any plant unless the physical appearance satisfies all the points described in the book.

The book also touches upon some common, easily-recognized, wild mushrooms. These are as much a part of the forager's world as are green plants. But again, never consume even a tiny amount of any mushroom without making absolutely, 100 percent certain, that it is the mushroom described in the book.

In fact, when handling mushrooms, always wash your hands before touching any mucous membrane. Also, when collecting, make sure to segregate different types of mushrooms so that they do not touch each other. You just can't be too careful in this regard.

That said, the mushrooms noted in this book, once identified, can pay off in many years of enjoyable harvesting and gourmet eating. The way to learn about mushrooms is easy…just learn one mushroom at a time. Study it inside and out. Read every book available. Better yet, take the mushroom and have a professional identify it for you. Then, it's welcome to the rewarding, highly-satisfying world of the wild mushroom hunter.

Finally, let me present the answer to the inevitable question of taste. It is tempting to say a plant tastes like spinach or perhaps, Swiss chard. In most cases, though, there are very few corresponding domestic vegetables that taste exactly like wild plants. Wild plants have their own taste and, as such, have value in their own right. As close as anyone can honestly come when describing how a wild plant tastes is to say that it is mild, hot, sweet, sour or bitter. Other than that, taste is subjective and, therefore, best experienced firsthand rather than described in so many words.

Not all the plants described here are edible and only some have medicinal value. But all have some use, a few of which may be surprising. If, after reading this book, you are "hooked" on learning more regarding Maine's wild plants, a trip to your local bookstore can prove useful. The new-found popularity of wild plants has spawned a huge flush (oops…it sounds as though I'm talking of wild mushrooms here. That isn't a bad analogy, though) of guidebooks. Not the least of which is my book, *Foraging New England*. While *Foraging New England* covers wild plants found in the general region, all of them occur in Maine and all photos are of Maine plants. As a general note, all books mentioned in this book have been listed with complete citations in the resources section at the end of the book.

I hope you enjoy your foray into the wonderful, fascinating world of useful, wild Maine plants.

Spring

Here in Maine, spring begins while, for all practical purposes, it is yet winter. But lengthening days and strengthening sunlight trigger a slow but steady awakening. Buds swell on shrubs and trees, sap flows in maples and birdsong takes on a new, more energetic dimension. And beneath lingering ice and snow, wild edible plants stir. It's my favorite season and though I grow older each year, springtime in Maine makes me oblivious to the passage of time.

Evening Primrose

As the March sun works its magic and melts snow from south-facing hillsides and gravel banks, it reveals one of the first wild edible plants of the new season, evening primrose, *Oenothera biennis.*

Here in Maine, with our short growing season, annual and biennial (biennials live about two years. Their progeny result from seed dropped by the parent plant) plants must go about the business of growing and setting seed all in the

Evening primrose, the source of a superb springtime root crop.

relatively short growing season of approximately five months. So it's little wonder that evening primrose begins the process as soon as it is free from winter ice and snow.

In very early spring, then, evening primrose presents us with several types of food. First, the young leaves make an interesting ingredient in a simple salad. More important, though, the root is a superb vegetable, similar in shape to a parsnip, but with a milder taste.

To begin, it is the first-year plant we seek, the one that began growing from seed one year ago. The roots of older plants tend toward woodiness and the leaves are usually too tough for eating. Our young evening primrose appear as they were last fall, when they stopped growing, preserved in-situ by a prison of ice. Look for a basal whorl of somewhat ovate leaves, wider near the ends than the middle and slightly pointed. These have a prominent midrib and are tinged with scarlet at the edges and near the ends.

As long as the leaves remain flattened, hugging the ground, the root remains tender and ideal for cooking. But once the leaves rise in response to strengthening, spring sunlight and the stalk, or stem begins growing, the root becomes tough. So we have only a brief window of opportunity for evening primrose. This, you will find, pretty much pertains to all our wild edible plants. When considering the short growing season mentioned above, the reason for a limited timeframe becomes abundantly clear.

The young leaves make an interesting ingredient in a simple salad.

Which brings up an interesting point. Beginning foragers face something of a hit-or-miss proposition. The growing season in Maine does not begin or end at the same time throughout the state. Instead, spring slowly creeps into southern regions sometime in March, while northern areas may need to wait a month or more to enjoy similar conditions. It all depends upon where in Maine the forager lives. Also, islands and the immediate coast have a far milder climate than inland. Even inland, the difference in climate between high elevations and low valleys is striking.

Locate evening primrose in late summer by its tall flowerstalk and small yellow flowers.

This underscores the importance of keeping either written or mental notes. When locating that patch of wild edible plants at just the right stage for harvest, make sure to mark the time and place well. This makes it easy to return the following year for a repeat performance.

Back, then, to our first spring plant—evening primrose. After locating evening primrose, dig the roots with a hand trowel. Note that evening primrose roots are white, with a trace of pink near the crown. Fortunately for harvesters, these plants usually grow in groups rather than singly. The reason being, the parent plant drops many dozens of seeds and they all fall fairly near each other. In fact, it is often easy to look about, after locating a stand of evening primrose and see the stiff, dried stalks of the parent plants.

Once dug, place the roots, with their leaves, in a container and take home for processing. Cut the top of the root in the same way you might cut the top off a carrot, leaving the leaves intact. Then select the smallest leaves and remove them for use as potherbs or in a salad.

Large roots should be peeled and smaller ones can simply be scrubbed under running water, my preferred method. Cook the roots by boiling, but first, slice them lengthwise to facilitate thorough cooking. When fork-tender, drain and serve with salt, pepper and butter.

Cattail Sprouts

Who isn't familiar with that denizen of ponds, swamps, marshes and roadside ditches, the common cattail? Cattails, *Typha latifolia,* are highly-efficient colonizers, popping up in new locations with perfect impunity. What's more, cattails frequently appear in world literature and art. British country people of the 19th century referred to the plant as bulrush and considered it the very same plant used to fashion a floating cradle for the infant Moses. The British also knew the common cattail as reed-mace. Rural Americans continue to refer to cattails as cat-of-nine-tails. And foragers know the ubiquitous cattail by a term popularized by Euell Gibbons, "supermarket of the swamps."

The last term listed above probably fits best, since common cattails provide a number of different food products. Four of these are described here according to the specific season for each different product. Some uses don't interest me, since they are not only energy-intensive, but also time-consuming. For me, foraging should come easy.

In spring, wild food harvesters seek cattail sprouts. Cattails vie with evening primrose for the title of first wild edible of springtime. In fact, a determined forager could, with some risk of hypothermia, harvest cattail products in midwinter, by cutting holes in the ice and pulling up the rootstalks. But such chilly and potentially risky endeavors are not recommended. So the prudent forager waits until early spring when dried, brown cattail leaves and stalks from last season protrude from newly thawed ponds and waterholes.

Young cattail plants, ready to harvest for their stalks.

Cattail sprouts are available as soon as the ice melts.

Even then, in early spring, cattail harvesters must dress warmly and also don rubber boots and even rubber gloves. That's because the first available cattail product is a short, white sprout that projects from the submerged rootstalk and must be pulled from the icy water before using. This is a starchy product and, as such, makes a somewhat crunchy and mild addition to wild salads. These sprouts are equally welcomed in stir-fry recipes.

For me, harvesting cattail sprouts entails putting on hip boots and, with long-handled spade in hand, walking out in the shallow section of a nearby pond. There, I work the point of my spade under a cattail root clump and, with one hand prying on the handle, grasp the plant with the other hand and apply steady pressure until the muck releases its grip on my plant, something often accompanied by a loud, slurping sound. It's a muddy, cold business but in late March, a very worthwhile one.

The sprouts don't require peeling, only careful washing in cold water. In fact, it pays to wash these several times, just for safety so as to remove any waterborne bacteria.

As a suggestion, cattail sprouts might go well with young, evening primrose leaves in that first, wild salad of the year. For me, such as this becomes food for the soul as well as for the body. Both seem to warrant equal attention after a long, cold winter.

Coltsfoot, A Dandelion Look-Alike

Coltsfoot, *Tussilago farfara,* serves Maine foragers as a bellwether plant. It's bright-yellow, dandelion-like flowers tell us that the time has come to look for a number of different wild edibles. Many of the early spring plants come into their own at this time.

Look for masses of yellow flowers on gravel banks and along south-facing roadsides and hillsides. Alfred Lord Tennyson penned the following verse in honor of sea pink, *Armeria maritima,* but it fits equally well to describe coltsfoot:

> *Wonder at the bonteous hours,*
> *The slow result of winter showers,*
> *You scarce can see the grass for flowers.*

Interestingly, lots of people confuse coltsfoot with dandelions. Every year in mid-April, it seems, someone announces that dandelions are in bloom. Of course that event doesn't normally happen for several weeks.

Coltsfoot gets its common name from the shape of its leaves. These are roughly shaped like a colt or horse's footprint. The scientific name, though, tells us something about its historical use. Tussis is Latin for "cough." This prompts me to mention that in most cases, common names of plants have little value, at least as far as telling us much about a plant's properties. In fact, common names are often misleading and, even worse, a number of unrelated plants share a com-

Coltsfoot, one of our earliest blooming wildflowers.

Coltsfoot signals the coming of spring.

mon name. Scientific names always, or almost always, offer a good deal of specific information about the plant. And even if we mispronounce them, the scientific name is far better overall than the common name, in that it is used and recognized worldwide, whereas common names might vary from region to region, even state to state.

Coltsfoot leaves, dried, are smoked as a treatment for lung conditions. All the same, smoking something to help the lungs seems counterproductive. Besides that, the plant contains certain alkaloids that are considered toxic, especially in large doses.

So for me, coltsfoot remains a pretty, spring wildflower, particularly beloved because it signals that finally and at long last, the time has come to get out and begin harvesting Maine's wonderful, wild edible plants.

Additionally, at least in Mid-Coast Maine, sea-run brook trout ascend tidal rivers and streams about the same time that coltsfoot blooms. So coltsfoot not only signals when various wild edible plants are ready, it also lets us know the best time to go fishing.

By the way, coltsfoot is another one of those wild plants that came here from across the sea. In fact, I was amazed to see a recent church bulletin. It featured a scenic photo of a barren, rocky mountainside in the Holy Land. And there, just as plain as could be, was a blooming coltsfoot.

Blunt-Leaved Dock

Still in early spring, around late April in the Mid-Coast region, foragers can expect to find blunt-leaved dock, a member of the *Rumex* tribe. We here in Maine have several types of dock, and separating the different types often leads to great frustration. Fortunately, all the various docks have similar properties and all offer fine eating, plus a walloping dose of vitamins.

The docks have another use, one that most country children were once aware of. Dock (supposedly) takes the sting out of nettle rash and also insect bites. Rubbing crushed dock on the affected spot and chanting, "Out nettle, in dock; nettle, nettle stung me" was the accepted procedure.

Blunt-leaved dock grows along streams and wet areas.

This use against rashes, nettle stings and insect bites was well-known in Great Britain in earlier days. Other medicinal properties were attributed to the various docks. A line in Browne's *Pastorals* reads: "And softly 'gan it bind, with dock-leaves and a slip of willow-rind." That alludes to dock's ability to heal wounds.

The first dock we find, then, in early spring, I have tentatively identified as blunt-leaved dock. This has wide, egg-shaped leaves and a prominent red midrib. The emerging leaves often wave to us from small brooks and tiny rivulets. In time, these vernal waterways will either dry completely or shrink to nothing but a trickle, leaving the resident docks high and dry.

Dock is closely related to buckwheat, as evidenced by the seeds. They are nearly identical to that cultivated grain crop. Interestingly, many of the wild plants that we so cherish occur on both sides of the Atlantic. People in Britain have known and used dock for untold centuries. It is supposed that the various docks were purposely brought to the New World. Such was the usefulness to people and such was the esteem that colonists conferred upon this common, unassuming wildling.

A book, *The Flowering Plants of Great Britain*, dated 1870 and signed, presumably, by the author, indicates that at least back then, the correct botanical name for what they called broad-leaved dock (this pretty closely resembles the blunt-leaved dock described here) was *Rumex obtusifolius*. But scientific names aside, this dock is tasty and very widespread. Seek it along streams, wet areas and especially, along the alluvial plain, that place where high water of winter has receded and deposited in its wake a coating of rich, sandy soil.

So when blackflies harrass us in earnest and spring peepers fill the night with their high-pitched chorus, it is time to seek blunt-leaved dock. Break off the leaves with your fingers and place in a basket or other suitable container. Then take home and rinse. Remove the stem, but leave the leaf otherwise intact.

To cook, bring a slight amount of water to a boil and drop the leaves in. Watch closely, since when the leaves turn a light shade of green, they are ready. It doesn't hurt much to undercook, but above all, do not overcook. Drain immediately and serve with butter, salt and pepper.

Dandelion

Common dandelion, *Taraxacum officinale,* is probably the best-known wild edible of all. Who hasn't at least heard that dandelions can be eaten? Interestingly, these are another of those transplanted, or alien, plants brought here from Britain. Did those old travelers bring dandelions on purpose? One wonders if they had the presence of mind to worry about transporting edible "weeds." Perhaps dandelion seeds in the hay brought over to feed livestock paved the way for the dandelion invasion that would quickly take place. However they arrived, dandelions quickly became well established.

It pains me to hear the host on my favorite gardening show explaining to

Dandelions are best harvested with the help of a simple hand tool.

callers how best to rid their lawns of dandelions. After all, I often travel many miles to dig dandelions from fields and pristine (no cats and dogs) lawns.

Early on, my own lawn lacked dandelions, a situation that I soon remedied by gathering the white, fluffy seedheads and, like a child, walked about blowing on them and letting them drift on the breeze, to finally populate my lawn with tasty dandelions.

Dandelions are another of those plants best harvested with the help of a simple hand tool. Dandelion diggers pop up in garden centers and hardware stores each spring. These are meant to help people rid their lawn of the "pesky weeds." They are equally as valuable to knowledgeable foragers who wish to pick not only dandelion leaves, but also the crowns and perhaps even part of the roots.

Dig dandelions in spring as soon as they become available. As the season progresses, the plants become increasingly bitter. Young, tender dandelions, though, strike me as sweet and mild.

Remember that even a little bit of root will serve to produce another dandelion to dig the following year. And that's a good thing for those of us who revel in eating dandelions.

Young, tender dandelion leaves make a tasty addition to any wild salad and the cooked leaves, along with the crown and any unopened buds, make a fine vegetable. Just place the leaves, crowns and buds in boiling water and turn the heat to medium. Keep picking them up with a fork and when they become tender, drain and serve. I like my dandelion greens with an accompaniment of butter, salt and pepper and sometimes, a dash of cider vinegar.

Dandelions keep well when frozen. I always put up a number of packages. It's easy, too. Just blanch in boiling water until the leaves wilt, perhaps for two minutes. Then drain and immerse in ice-cold water. When cool, pack in plastic freezer bags and the product is ready for storage. When it is time to use the frozen dandelions, remove from the plastic bags and place directly in boiling water and cook until the leaves separate.

Speaking of freezing, now is a good time to mention an easy and inexpensive method I found to store plants in the freezer. For years, plastic freezer bags were sold with a twist-tie closure. These older bags were thinner than those sold today. The procedure in years past was to blanch, drain and cool the product, pack it in a freezer bag and squeeze every trace of air from the bag, something made simple by the thin, flexible bags. At that point, a twist tie kept the thing sealed. A number of such bags, ready for freezing, could then go into a larger, storage bag for extra protection.

Today, though, freezer bags are much stiffer and thicker. This makes it impossible to squeeze all the air out after filling. Also, the thick sides do not adhere to the food and thus allow for more trapped air. Finally, the bags no longer come with a twist tie, but a sliding closure. This, too, contributes to more trapped air and ultimately, freezer burn. There is an inexpensive way to circumvent this problem, however.

Instead of placing my products directly in the new-style freezer bags, I first put them in fold-top sandwich bags. These are quite thin and flexible and adhere to the moist product inside, thus preventing trapped air. Now, after folding the top and squeezing out any air and also extra moisture, the filled sandwich bags go in the modern, zipper-type bags. I like to use gallon-size freezer bags for storing my single-portion sandwich bags. I can put a dozen meals worth in one freezer bag. This also keeps the product together, making it easy to select exactly the desired plant.

Sandwich bags are dirt-cheap and they work better, when used in conjunction with regular, freezer bags, than anything I have yet found.

Ostrich Fern Fiddleheads

All ferns enter a so-called "fiddlehead" stage, but not all fiddleheads make good eating. Fiddleheads are the crosier, or curled-up tip of an emerging fern. In Maine, we seek only one (this despite the argument that bracken ferns are good) fiddlehead, that of the ostrich fern, *Matteuccia strathiopteris*.

Even old-time fiddleheaders have difficulty predicting exactly when any particular patch of fiddleheads will offer crosiers of just the perfect size. Cool, cloudy weather can inhibit growth to a great degree and conversely, a few days of warm sunshine might cause the fiddleheads to erupt in only a day. For this reason, hopeful foragers make several, fruitless trips to their favorite fiddleheading spots before finding everything just right.

Fiddleheads grow in semi-shaded, moist woodlands and also along fertile streamsides. Look for them in the rich, sandy loam left by the retreating high water of early spring.

These ferns grow in clumps, and not all the fiddleheads erupt at the same time. This makes it possible to go to a spot, pick a number of fiddleheads and return within a few days, only to find an equal number ready for picking.

Young fiddleheads are ready for harvest as soon as they can be grasped between thumb and forefinger and snapped from their parent clump. Most fiddleheaders prefer these short, nearly stemless crosiers. However, they remain good to eat, sweet and tender, even up to five or six inches tall. As long as the top remains coiled, the fiddlehead is fine. In fact, the stem tastes great too, so practical foragers sometimes pick relatively tall fiddleheads so that they can have a meal of the stems. At the very least, don't discard the stems. Chop them up into inch-long lengths, if desired, and cook them along with the crosiers.

A papery, brown parchment covers the immature fern and this presents problems for unwary foragers. This parchment contains tannin, which turns cooking water black and imparts a bitter taste to the fiddleheads. For that rea-

The fiddlehead crosier bears a striking resemblance to the headstock of a fiddle. They later evolve into the mature ostrich fern seen in the lower picture.

son, it must be removed before eating. Far too many foragers simply pick their fiddleheads, take them home and rinse them under a stream of cold water. This removes less than half the parchment and causes the rest to adhere to the plant like grim death. For that reason, proper procedure dictates that the parchment be removed while the fiddlehead is yet dry.

I like to tweak fiddleheads with a finger before snapping them from the clump. This simple act shakes off a large amount of parchment. Then, back at home, I spread the fiddleheads out on a picnic table and allow the wind to blow the remaining parchment away. On calm days, a hand-held fan serves to winnow the parchment from the fiddleheads.

Only after thorough dry cleaning should you wash fiddleheads. In fact, if they are to be stored in the refrigerator (they keep well for a week or more), don't wash until ready to use. However, if the fiddleheads begin to wilt before you can prepare them, a quick rinse in ice-cold water firms them and helps extend their shelf life.

Cook fiddleheads as you would broccoli, by steaming or boiling. The cooked vegetable goes well with salt, pepper and butter. Cold, cooked fiddleheads make a unique and tasty salad ingredient. But don't eat them raw, since raw fiddleheads have a profound, laxative effect.

Besides just boiling, fiddleheads lend themselves to a number of interesting recipes. Look in the recipe section of this book for more fiddlehead-cooking ideas.

Orpine

Anyone who grows the rock garden perennial Sedum "Autumn Joy," will instantly recognize wild orpine, a close relative. Orpine, *Sedum purpureum*, prefers poor, gravelly soil. It grows on roadside banks and also on field edges. In early spring (about the time that coltsfoot blooms), the young, leaf clumps push up through the ground and, when they are no more than an inch or two tall, are a fine trail nibble.

Many times while trout fishing, I have eaten my fill of young orpine leaves and considered it my very good fortune to have found such fare there for the taking.

Add orpine to your salad or enjoy as a trail nibble.

The young leaves are fleshy, thick and coarsely toothed. In addition to their use as a trail nibble, they are excellent in salads (have you kept track of how many wild, early-spring salad ingredients we have noted thus far?) and also boiled for a short time.

The tubers, which look something like tiny sweet potatoes, are another edible root crop. These are fairly small, though, and I don't like bothering with them, preferring to wait until I can locate the larger tubers of groundnut. But for curiosity's sake, don't hesitate to pick a number of these little tubers, take them home for a good scrubbing and finally, for a trial on the dinner table. Just boil them until tender.

As the season progresses and orpine grows taller, the leaves lose their mild flavor and instead take on a rather strong taste. Therefore, they are best enjoyed during their own brief season.

Curled Dock

A nameless author, writing in ancient England, referred to the various docks as, "exceeding strengthening to the liver, and procures good blood, being as wholesome a pot-herb as any growing in the garden; yet such is the nicety of our time, forsooth! that women will not put it in a pot because it makes the pottage black: Pride and ignorance, a couple of monsters in the creation, preferring nicety before health!"

My gosh, I wonder what would happen to that writer today if he said such a thing. It would not go easy for him. Besides that, the idea of some "weed" being good for the liver and the blood raises some questions. On the other hand, the docks are rich in vitamin C and also contain large amounts of vitamin A. Accordingly, modern herbalists often consider dock a good "blood purifier." Perhaps those old-time writers were not so far off base after all.

Knowing that a delicious wild food contains beneficial vitamins makes them all the more desirable. To that end, curled dock, *Rumex crispus*, has a regular place on my menu, as long as the supply lasts.

General aspects of the docks were described earlier, under Blunt-Leaved Dock. Curled dock differs from the blunt-leaved variety in that, the plant grows on both moist and also somewhat drier ground. Indeed, some old-time Maine homes have well-established clumps of curled dock on their front lawns, evidence of the esteem our ancestors held for this common plant. Curled dock also establishes itself in drainage ditches and these may present the best locations for locating a group of plants.

Next, curled dock takes its common name from the general shape of the leaves. These are long and slender, lance-shaped, with curled, irregular margins or leaf edges. In truth, this plant is well named.

Curled dock is a vitamin-laden potherb.

I pick dock leaves well into late spring and even early summer, as long as the plant keeps producing new, tender leaves. Leaves up to ten inches or slightly longer, as long as they are deep green and tender, make a fine potherb. When the leaves take on a yellow tint, they are too tough for use.

Just snip the tender young leaves, take home and rinse and then steam in a slight amount of water. As with blunt-leaved dock, do not overcook. Drain and serve with butter, salt, pepper and a dash of cider vinegar.

By the way, if you develop a taste for curled dock and would like for it to grow on your own land, just wait until late summer and pick a handful of the dried seeds. These are easy to spot, being on a tall seed spike. Then, select a damp area along a lawn or field edge and cast the seeds. In a few years, you should have a fine supply of curled dock.

Japanese Knotweed

Japanese knotweed, *Polygonum cuspidatum* the bane of homeowners everywhere. Imported from Japan as an ornamental, the plant has, during the last one hundred or so years, become widespread throughout Maine and, indeed, the rest of the country.

As a dedicated forager, it amuses me to hear of the pains people go through to rid their property of Japanese knotweed. Of course any plant that has had a one hundred-year head start must require some determination to eradicate. But, I always ask, why do people wish to kill the plant anyway? Don't they appreciate its beauty, the attractive, bamboo-like internodes and the feathery, whitish-green, flowers? And, too, don't people know what a wonderful food item this makes? The answer in most cases seems to be a definite no.

Japanese knotweed spreads rampantly, but only when disturbed. The large stands we normally encounter are mostly from the original plantings. Given their advanced age, it's little wonder that they cover such a large area. When left alone, Japanese knotweed seems content to spread at a snails-pace. Only

Find young emerging shoots of Japanese knotweed amongst last year's dry stalks. These soon reach a usable size for cooking. Bottom photo shows knotweed ready for steaming.

when the town road crew freshens a ditch containing knotweed does the plant become such a successful pioneer. Or, perhaps, when a distressed homeowner attempts to till the plants under, does Japanese knotweed overstep its bounds.

So if we can't beat Japanese knotweed, it just makes all kinds of sense to use it to the fullest. That means harvesting the young shoots and having them for dinner. The shoots are hollow, making them easy to snap with one hand. As long as the shoot makes a distinct popping sound when snapped, it is probably tender enough for table use.

Select shoots that easily bend. These are the tenderest. Early on, when yellow coltsfoot blossoms shine in roadside ditches, knotweed shoots erupt from the ground. When these are five or six inches tall, they are ready for harvest. But even when the shoots attain a height of several feet, they can still be used, if we pick only the tender, flexible tip.

Admittedly, some wild plants are tedious to pick. Not so for Japanese knotweed. In only a few minutes a person can easily pick a half-bushel or more. Just fill a canvas bag or a large basket with as many Japanese knotweed shoots as you care to deal with. Then bring them home for table use. Excess shoots keep well in the crisper drawer of a refrigerator. In fact, this is one time when a plastic storage bag comes in handy. Just don't close or seal the bag and your knotweed tips will remain in good shape in the refrigerator for up to one week.

To use, first rinse and then cut the shoots to a length that will easily fit in a frying pan. Put about one inch of water in the pan and bring to a boil. Do this only after the rest of your meal is ready to serve. Place the rinsed shoots in the boiling water, turn down to simmer and by the time everything else is on the table, a few minutes later perhaps, the knotweed will have turned a lighter shade of green and will be tender, ready to serve.

Drain well and serve with butter, salt and pepper. Japanese knotweed can be used in desserts and also in a wondrously flavorful chutney. Find these recipes in the recipe section of this book.

This almost universally-despised "weed" is, indeed, one of my very favorite wild edible plants.

Stinging Nettles

As a practical matter, I don't specifically seek stinging nettles and you will soon see why. Nettles grow on the alluvial plain, that fertile strip along river and streamsides. And since nettles come around about the time ostrich fern fiddleheads are ready, I combine my fiddleheading trip with a bit of nettle harvesting.

To that end, I always carry leather gloves. Stinging nettles, *Urtica dioica*, didn't get their common name for nothing. Nettle leaves and stems bristle with thousands of tiny stinging needles. The scientific name comes from the

Stinging nettles are aptly named as you can see by the numerous spines.

Latin, *uro*, which means "to burn." And nettle is derived from the Anglo-Saxon, *netel*, for "needle."

Fortunately, the stinging aspect of stinging nettles is dispelled upon cooking. So, upon locating a stand of nettles (they seldom grow singly, but rather in fairly large colonies), break off the young plants, using both, gloved hands. A pair of scissors might help, but that means carrying extra gear, something that doesn't appeal to me. When nettle plants exceed six inches or so, they become somewhat tough and even a bit gritty. Stick to the small, tender shoots.

Nettles, besides having the obvious, stinging hairs, have coarsely toothed leaves, wide at the bottom and roundly pointed at the end. The leaves grow opposite each other on the stem, making them easy to identify.

Use leather gloves when harvesting nettles.

In the field, store your nettles in a bag separate from other plants. Later, at home, spread (still using gloves) the nettles out and discard any foreign material and look for roots clinging to the shoots. Snip the roots if any are present. Then rinse the nettles and either prepare immediately or store in the refrigerator as per Japanese knotweed.

Cooking nettles is a snap. Put only about a half-inch of water in a saucepan. After rinsing the nettles, make sure not to shake them, so as to allow any clinging water to remain. When the water in the saucepan simmers, drop the wet nettles in and cook slowly until the nettles become fork tender. This may take up to ten minutes. I sometimes add just the tiniest pinch of baking soda in order to speed cooking time. Baking soda also tenderizes the plant, something to remember when cooking other greens.

When tender, drain the nettles, reserving the liquid for other uses. Serve with butter, salt, pepper and cider vinegar.

Allow the cooking liquid, which by now has turned a fairly dark green, to cool and then place in a plastic container and either place in the refrigerator or the freezer. This is the main ingredient for a delicious soup, the recipe for which appears in the recipe section.

Nettles have a long and honorable history. Another transplant to North America, nettles were widely used in Britain and Europe. Sir Walter Scott spoke of country people outside of Glasgow, Scotland, forcing nettles as their "spring kail." Kail, here, being a general term for green potherb. Forcing means to artificially induce plant growth, something usually done well before the plant would naturally become usable.

The Scots, and also inhabitants of various nations on the Continent, made use of nettle fiber for cloth, the likes of which was renowned for its durability.

Purple Trillium

For the most part, the various trilliums should not be picked but rather appreciated as beautiful, ephemeral wildflowers. But purple trillium, *Trillium erectum,* often grows in vast colonies, enough to allow for limited, judicious picking. Even then, I recommend taking only one leaf from any one plant. This in no way harms the plant and insures that the colony will continue as always, unharmed by this light harvesting.

The purple trilliums (all parts of trilliums are in groups of three, including leaves, petals and bracts) on my woodlot have suffered no apparent harm, even after many years of me selectively harvesting their leaves. Make sure the plants you select are truly purple trillium, rather than the more rare, painted trillium, which has white petals trimmed with scarlet at their base. Trillium leaves are broad in the middle and roundly pointed at the end.

Herbalists have long used trilliums as medicine. Such a use requires a more extensive harvest, something I seek to avoid.

One of the first wildflowers of spring, trilliums show up around late April, well before leaves on deciduous trees have matured. Trilliums are designed to do their growing and flowering in the filtered light of early spring.

Anyway, after locating a large stand of trilliums and handpicking enough individual leaves for a serving, take pains to keep the leaves in a cool loca-

Purple trillium has edible leaves. Try them lightly steamed.

tion, out of direct sunlight, or they will quickly wilt and lose their quality. At home, rinse the leaves and cook in a slight amount of water, only until the leaf wilts and turns a more pronounced shade of green. Do not overcook. Drain and serve with the usual salt, pepper and butter.

Purple trilliums are not a plant that I pick in quantity. Instead, I relish the one or two helpings that nature provides for me each spring. A side dish of steamed trillium leaves has become a regular rite of spring for me. The leaves also can be used in a salad. I prefer them cooked.

Regarding taste, I can only describe steamed or boiled trillium leaves as generally mild, but with a slight hint of piquancy.

To my knowledge, no studies exist to tell us what vitamins or minerals are contained in trillium leaves. But it seems quite likely that the dark green leaves must contain significant amounts of both vitamin A and vitamin C. I'd stack them up against commercially-raised spinach any day.

Trout Lily

Sometime in late April or early May, trout lilies, *Erythronium americanum,* put on a spectacular show along Maine roadsides and in sparse woodlands where sunlight leaps and dances. A native member of the lily family, *Liliceae,* trout lilies please the palate as well as the eye.

In my part of Maine, trout lilies appear at a time when most other wildflowers have yet to mature. It's a time when red, fuzzy flowers adorn maple trees (yes,

Trout lilies grow in often huge, dense colonies. The leaves are mottled with brown splotches, reminiscent of the markings on the side of a brook trout.

maple trees have flowers, but most people mistake them for leaf buds) and the first ostrich fern fiddleheads of the year break through the sandy soil along streamsides.

It's also a time when, spurred on by warming water temperatures, this ephemeral plant's namesake, trout, become ravenously hungry. Simply put, it's a lovely, exhilarating and magnificent time of year, a time when wild plants erupt in abundance. Things in nature move fast now, so for those who would avail themselves of the sight and also, the taste, of trout lilies, there is no time to waste.

Trout lilies grow in often huge, dense colonies. Their requirements are few, but absolutely necessary. These include dappled springtime shade and loose, moist woodland soil. Trout lilies have a stem that measures anywhere between six and twelve inches. Two oblong-to-lance-shaped leaves, roundly pointed on the end, emerge from the base of the stem. These leaves are usually of unequal length, flat, shiny, smooth and of a pleasing, dark green color. The leaves are mottled with brown splotches, reminiscent of the markings on the side of a brook trout.

The trout lily flower stem appears from between the leaves. This bears a single, yellow, nodding flower. The flower rises just slightly above the leaves.

Trout lilies grow from a rather small, deeply-buried corm (this corm is edible, but attempts to dig it with a hand trowel are usually ineffectual) and the corm, as with so many other plants in the lily family, produces side shoots from which spring new trout lilies.

Since the corm takes so much effort to harvest, I consider it more of an emergency food rather than a staple. The leaves, though, have considerable value as a potherb. These are easily harvested and even simpler to prepare.

Although it does little or no harm to pick a few pints of leaves from a large colony of trout lilies, something in me says to only harvest one leaf from each plant. Accordingly, I pick the largest leaf from an individual plant and leave the smaller to continue the process of photosynthesis.

When harvesting, take care to use only a basket or canvas bag so that air can circulate freely and the leaves don't become damp from condensation. Then, back home, rinse and drain the leaves prior to cooking. Treat trout lily leaves as a delicate potherb, meaning only cook for a few minutes in a scant amount of boiling water. Drain and serve as any potherb.

The delicate taste of trout lily leaves recommends them to even the most refined palate. I consider these one of the finer springtime treats and given their brief window of availability (I find them best before they set flower), prefer to have only one or two pickings and to eat these fresh, the day they are harvested.

Trout lily leaves may lend themselves to various methods of preservation, but I discourage people from harvesting them in such large quantities. Better to appreciate the ephemeral nature of these springtime treasures. For me, that means sampling them when in season and then patiently waiting for the next season to roll around.

Jewelweed

By late April or early May, jewelweed, *Impatiens capensis*, is ready to harvest. Well, at least that holds true for the jewelweed on my Mid-Coast Maine property. Remember for all these plants, the calendar surges ahead and drops back, according to location and also current climate conditions.

Jewelweed precedes ostrich fern fiddleheads and stinging nettles by nearly one week. Again, that's just what happens in my locale. Jewelweed grows in moist, shady areas. This includes edges of driveways and lawns, drainage ditches and almost any place where it can keep its feet damp and find protection from the hot sun.

Since an extensive stand of jewelweed grows only about 100 feet from my home office, it takes me only a short while to determine whether or not the plant has grown to a point where I can perform an initial harvest. But it seems as though the watched pot never boils, because day-to-day growth appears imperceptible. And then, as if overnight, my jewelweed reaches a stage where it can provide that first, welcomed meal.

Jewelweed wilts quickly, so I make certain not to allow it to languish in my collecting basket. As with so many other wildlings, the small plants cook in only a few minutes, so I prepare the main part of my meal first and prepare my jewelweed last. Just a few minutes of simmering in a saucepan with an inch or

Young jewelweed, a tender potherb of early spring.

so of water are sufficient to cook young jewelweed plants. Drain and serve as any other green vegetable.

Notice that I keep referring to the entire plant rather than just the leaves. When jewelweed is between two and four inches tall, it is perfect for harvest. Just snip the plant, taking care not to pull it up by the root. If some roots still cling, just break them off. If the stand is thick enough and other plants and weeds don't interfere, a scissors can come in handy for cutting young jewelweed plants at their base. Either way, take stem and leaves, minus roots.

The best way to locate young jewelweed in early spring is to spot the seed leaves, or cotyledons. These are the primordial leaves of annuals and biennials. They are thick, fleshy and generally rounded, but with a single notch, or depression on the edge. Jewelweed has a twin set of these leaves. As a matter of interest, these are edible too, but quite tedious to pick. I have made a meal, though, of jewelweed cotyledons. Also, they are nice in a salad.

Having spotted the cotyledons, watch for the emerging adult. Jewelweed leaves are somewhat ovate and roundly pointed at the tips, with very coarse (but not sharp) edges. The stem is succulent, water-filled and appears almost translucent. These features, plus their "unwettable" nature, should serve to make a positive identification. Unwettable, by the way, refers to the plants water-repellent properties. Even immersing in water cannot wet or even dampen jewelweed.

As with so many other wild plants, I enjoy jewelweed best when in season. Each spring, for about two weeks, I have regular servings of jewelweed. Each season has its treasures, and in early to mid-spring, jewelweed is surely one of our more precious, natural treasures.

Large-Leaved Aster

As May progresses and male woodpeckers drum on hollow trees in order to attract females and warn off competing males, large-leaved asters, *Aster macrophyllus,* appear in sun-dappled woodland edges. Its value as a potherb comes before the leaf fully opens, or unfurls. Later, the leaves become too thick and tough for table use.

In late summer, the plant sends up a seedstalk, complete with small and rather insignificant pale, violet flowers. This stalk remains pretty much intact throughout the winter and provides a signal for foragers to search the forest floor for young-of-the-year, large-leaved asters.

In summer, the basal, or lower leaves sometimes attain a width of up to eight inches. Upper leaves, though, are much smaller. But in spring, when the erect, still-furled leaves erupt, often lifting or displacing dead leaves and other litter from the ground, the new seedstalk has yet to develop.

These plants grow in often immense colonies. Picking a small basket of individual

The still-furled leaves of the large-leaved aster are at the perfect stage for picking.

leaves does not harm the group in the least. Even as the earliest leaves open and assume that trademark heart-shape, younger leaves continue to shoot up.

Only pick leaves that have yet to unfurl. The closely-wrapped individuals are best, but slightly-open ones work fine, too.

In any stage, the leaves have coarse teeth and a basal notch, giving it its signature Valentine-heart shape.

Again, this plant offers its best use during a brief harvest season. For plants on my woodlot, that is only about one week. But that's fine, because that week-long festival of free woodland bounty instills a great sense of anticipation for next year's aster season. The wheel of nature turns slowly but surely and the circle remains yet unbroken.

One of my favorite wild plant locations—a small woodland located on top of a bluff overlooking Penobscot Bay—has one of the largest colonies of large-leaved asters I have ever seen. I usually visit this site in late spring. By then, leaves on deciduous trees have matured and the asters are almost completely shaded. Even on the hottest days, this place offers cool ocean breezes amid luxuriant shade—a perfect setting for a casual, wild-plant foraging trip.

So pick a good number of leaves of the large-leaved aster and, after rinsing, bring water in a saucepan to a slow roll and cook for up to ten minutes or just until the leaves become fork-tender and assume a light color. Drain well and serve as for other green potherbs.

False Solomon's Seal

Like the country kid who quite naturally picks a stalk of Timothy and begins nibbling, I habitually chew on the raw stems of false Solomon's seal. False Solomon's seal, *Smilacina racemosa*, becomes ready for use at the same time as so many other springtime wild edibles. Again, this is another plant that provides a relatively short window of opportunity for foragers.

While the tender young shoots are said to make a good cooked vegetable and the rootstocks, after extensive preparation, supposedly make good table fare when boiled, neither of these uses excite me. It's simply too much trouble to collect enough shoots for cooking and it's much too difficult to soak the rootstocks in lye (the typical, prescribed procedure) before cooking. For me, false Solomon's seal is first and foremost a delicious seasonal trail nibble.

False Solomon's seal grows in cool, damp woodland loam and on the alluvial plain. The path to the streamside where I pick ostrich fern fiddleheads is edged with lush stands of false Solomon's seal. Who can blame me, then, if I tarry a bit picking and nibbling on the young, tender shoots?

People who buy most of their produce from a supermarket often stop at a table and try the free samples offered by different companies. For me, nature provides the samples and False Solomon's seal is just one of them.

Look for a zigzag-shaped stem, up to two feet or more long, with prominently veined, alternate lance-shaped leaves. Don't dig the plant, but with a jackknife (another indispensable tool for foragers), trim the shoot close to the ground. You'll

The shoots of false Solomon's seal make a fine trail nibble.

know if your shoots have gone past their prime, because they will make for tough chewing. But when they are just right, they provide a crisp and crunchy, sweet trail nibble, just the perfect complement to a morning spent walking the springtime woods, hunting the wild edible plants of Maine.

Wild Oats

As with many other wild plants of springtime, wild oats, *Smilacina racemosa,* delight the spirit as well as the palate. Who can resist a closer examination of the forked stem and tubular yellow flowers that hang, or depend, from the graceful leaf stems? A hand magnifier does much to help illustrate the beauty of this flower's exotic-looking design.

Wild oats grow in the same places and at the same time as false Solomon's seal, ostrich fern fiddleheads, blunt-leaved dock and stinging nettles. And they are best eaten in the same manner as false Solomon's seal.

I don't know anyone, other than myself, who routinely eats wild oats or, for that matter, false Solomon's seal. Both make perfectly fine trail nibbles, but neither offers the bulk and weight that so many people prefer in their wild edibles. For me, though, these tender, fleeting visions of springtime in my beloved Maine woodlands are worth every bit as much as other wild foods.

As an interesting insight, the second half of the botanical name for wild oats, *sessifolia*, says just everything about the plant. *Sessile* means that the leaves lack their own stalk and attach directly to the stem. *Folia* simply means foliage. Look at wild oats and see how the leaves do, in fact, attach to the plant stem, minus a stem of their own.

In nearly every instance, the scientific or botanical name of any plant imparts more useful information than the common name. Besides, it's fun learning these. It's like taking on a second language without having to sit in class. So I suggest that anyone with a few minutes to spare take time and ponder these two-part names. A familiarity with Greek or Latin isn't necessary, either, although it does help.

Use wild oats in the same way as false Solomon's seal.

Clintonia

Clintonia, *Clintonia borealis*, offers cucumber-tasting leaves in early May. As with large-leaved aster, the leaves are only usable when folded. As soon as they open and spread out, the taste becomes overly strong.

Clintonia is an exception to my remarks regarding the usefulness of botanical names. The first half of this member of the lily family's name was chosen in honor of De Witt Clinton, then governor of the state of New York. The second part, *borealis*, simply tells us that the plant grows in northern regions, not very helpful or definitive.

Unfortunately, the common name tells us nothing about this plant's table qualities, something that puzzles me greatly. Here we have a plant that tastes, in its raw state, precisely like cucumbers and yet that fact doesn't appear in the common name. Even worse, Clintonia has several common names, one being "corn lily." It is impossible for me to determine even the slimmest relationship between corn, or maize, and this diminutive springtime flower. So I return to my original statement. Common names are not worth much.

For future reference, if (and I don't list these here, preferring to keep things short and neat) a botanical name ends with "L", that's a reference to *Carolus Linnaeus*. *Linnaeus* designed the two-parted system of naming plants that we call binominal nomenclature. The first part of the name tells us the genus, the second the species.

But on to the wonders of Clintonia. The plant cannot tolerate full sun, nor can it survive in total shade. So it grows and thrives in the dappled spring sunlight, along woodland edges. The treeline along my driveway has lots of Clintonia growing, and that's where I pick my supply. It's easy to carry a collecting basket during the long walk to the mailbox and stop halfway there to check

out Clintonia. In fact, this strip of land has so many great wild plants that often it takes me an hour just to check my mail, a pleasant situation, indeed.

Clintonia serves as a trail nibble and a salad ingredient, where it takes the place of store-bought cucumbers. I've found

Clintonia tastes best when still tightly furled.

When fully-developed Clintonia becomes too strong for use.

that its best use comes when cut up into thin slices and sprinkled over a salad, where it adds just the right amount of pure cucumber flavor.

This brings up an interesting point. I'm not aware that anyone has ever isolated the principal in cucumbers that gives them their unique taste. But if that procedure were performed, odds are that the same ingredient would also exist in Clintonia.

Clintonia has two and sometimes three upright, shiny, broad leaves. When these leaves first erupt from the forest duff, they bear the appearance of neatly-folded dinner napkins, sitting upright in their napkin holders. As long as the leaves retain this configuration they are prime for picking.

In time, the leaves mature and that transformation reminds me of a moth or butterfly shedding its cocoon or chrysalis and emerging a much different creature. Mature Clintonia leaves are broad and shiny, with a prominent midrib. At that point, the six- to eight-inch, naked flowerstalk appears, bearing an average of three bell-shaped yellow flowers. Large stands of Clintonia make a striking sight at this time, one well worth stopping and admiring.

Following the flowers, later in summer, come the dark-blue berries. These should not be eaten, as they have a reputation for being toxic or, as Edgar T. Wherry so dryly put it, "rather poisonous."

Taken as a whole, Clintonia gives us a fine seasoning for our salads in early spring and in late spring and into summer, a handsome wildflower for our viewing pleasure. How can any wild plant do more?

Wintercress

Not all of Maine's edible wild plants live in woodland or even rural settings. Many are quite at home in suburbs and even in towns and cities. Wintercress, *Barbarea vulgaris*, serves to exemplify the adaptability of so many great wild plants.

The plant's scientific name, *Barbarea*, refers to Saint Barbara's Day, the fourth day of December. In regions south of Maine and also in the European countries from which wintercress originated, it was said that the plant was one of the few available to pick and eat at that time of year. The word *vulgaris* simply means common.

Country people, myself included, used to refer to wintercress as "mustard greens." This is a bit misleading, though, because while the plant resembles the *brassicas*, it is not one of them. It is, though, a crucifer, which alludes to the four-petaled flowers. No matter what we call it, wintercress provides us with a flavorful product, one that lasts over a longer period of time than most.

In early spring, the young leaves make a salad ingredient as well as a potherb for cooking. Later, the flower buds set on and I consider these one of the finer wild foods. Since the buds don't all ripen at once, that allows for a fairly long, perhaps two weeks or so, window of opportunity for picking.

Once, a small river in Mid-Coast Maine had everything needed to keep me

Use wintercress leaves in salads and as a cooked vegetable. Unopened flower buds when boiled or steamed, have a crisp texture.

coming back on a regular basis. Mayflies hatched there in great profusion and brown trout lined up on the edges of flows, lazily eating the flies as they drifted past. I caught and released countless fish that season. And as a topping to it all, wintercress grew on the sandy shore. Often, I would kill a trout to take home for supper and then go and harvest a bag of wintercress buds. Lacking any further ingredients, these two articles combined to make a perfectly delicious meal.

Another time, I was asked to host a wild plant walk in Maine's north woods. Knowing that shady, dense forests do not hold much of a wild plant bounty, I surreptitiously reconnoitered a nearby town. There, on a gravel bank on state-owned property, grew a huge colony of wintercress. Lots of other useful plants grew there too, making a success out of what might otherwise have been a relatively fruitless plant walk.

High Vitamin C content is just one of the benefits of this wild vegetable.

It pains me to admit it, but I often come close to missing out on wintercress. Springtime in Maine holds so many wonders that it seems like an impossibility to see, pick and taste every edible wild plant. In the case of wintercress, the plant gives us a second chance, as it were. The bright yellow flowers remind me to go and check for unopened buds. And most of the time, enough closed buds remain for me to harvest a substantial amount.

Wintercress grows to two feet tall. The lower leaves have separate lobes, with rounded ends and bear a slight resemblance to watercress leaves. The upper leaves are roughly toothed and clasp the stem. Buds develop into a spike atop the plant. Later, when seedpods develop, they are erect, parallel to the stem.

To cook, place the unopened buds (don't worry if a few have opened, since they won't hurt a thing) in boiling water and cook for three or four minutes. Drain and serve with butter, salt, pepper and if desired, a dash of cider vinegar. The leaves can be cooked and eaten the same way. Make sure to pick only the young, tender leaves. If you have some extra bacon strips, try cooking and chopping them up into small bits and sprinkling over your cooked wintercress leaves. It makes an interesting addition.

The late Euell Gibbons, whose writing and philosophy influenced so many, had a number of his favorite wild plants analyzed for vitamin content. Wintercress was one of these. Gibbons took a quantity of wintercress to the lab at Penn State University to have it checked and the results were quite impressive. These tests revealed an average of 152 milligrams of vitamin C per 100 grams of fresh wintercress leaves and 5,067 international units of vitamin A per one hundred grams of leaf. This far exceeds the vitamin content for many of our favorite cultivated vegetables.

Eating wild plants provides a way for us to have a steady intake of important vitamins without having to buy and take commercially-prepared vitamin products. Eating healthy seems an easy thing to do when we incorporate wholesome, tasty wild plants into our diet.

Garlic Mustard

A newcomer to Maine, garlic mustard has begun to present itself at scattered locations throughout the state. And with each passing year, the garlic-scented biennial appears in more and more new locations.

My first encounter with garlic mustard, *Alliaria petiolata*, came while leading a plant walk in coastal Maine. A participant spotted the frilly leaves first and asked me what it was. I had never seen this plant before but knew immediately, from seeing photos of it, that it was Garlic mustard. Picking and crushing the

Garlic mustard can be substituted in recipes calling for garlic cloves.

plant gave me all the proof I needed to tell participants in my walk that it was garlic mustard.

Garlic mustard is native to Europe, Britain and Asia and was a favorite plant of the English, who used it in recipes and as medicine. Early settlers brought garlic mustard to the New World and planted it so they could have easy access to its garlic-scented leaves and other plant parts for use as food and medicine. While the colonists didn't realize it, garlic mustard, as do all mustards, contains good amounts of Vitamin C and A. Garlic mustard also contains other healthful ingredients such as sulphenes.

Today, garlic mustard has spread of its own volition, and we find it throughout the Northeast and Midwest. Maine, probably because of its geography, was among the last to experience the garlic mustard invasion. The plant is now on Maine's invasive species list. Cultivation, sale or propagation of garlic mustard is prohibited. But as the plant spreads so easily on its own, placing it on a list of outlawed plants seems at best an exercise in futility.

Other states have waged total war against garlic mustard. Indiana, for instance, considers garlic mustard as one of its ten most destructive invasive species. That's because garlic mustard self-seeds so readily that it quickly takes over, effectively out-competing native plants. People in other states get together for garlic-pulling days in an attempt to eradicate the plant. But it's a guerrilla war at best, and thus far, garlic mustard has managed to stay on the winning side.

Look for garlic mustard along hedges or wood edges. In Grand Lake Stream, Maine, garlic mustard infests roadside ditches. I predict that eventually, garlic mustard will appear along the riparian habitat where ostrich ferns and stinging nettles live since rich, damp soil seems much to its liking.

But as with so many other non-natives, garlic mustard has many uses, making it a worthy candidate for inclusion in this book, Useful Wild Plants of Maine.

Garlic mustard is equally at home in recipes as clove-type garlic, both having an identical flavor. I've used it in salads as a garnish, with very good results. It excels as an add-on in stir-fries. The uses of garlic mustard are only limited by our imagination.

Garlic mustard, being a biennial, has a different appearance during its first year than in its second year. First-year plants remain fairly short, no more than six or seven inches high. And that's when the plant is at its best for use as a food. Second-year plants reach up to 3 feet before producing seeds and then dying. Second-year garlic mustard plants hold plenty of small, white, four-petaled blossoms, typical of all plants in the mustard family.

Began looking for garlic mustard in late April. Plants will only be a few inches high then, but that's fine because it's always easy to pick a good amount. Look for large, somewhat triangular-shaped, extremely, coarsely toothed leaves.

Common blue violet is more than just a pretty spring wildflower.

The leaves exhibit a wide, deep and distinct venation pattern. Pick the leaves, blossoms and immature seedpods, since these are all tender during the first year.

As with so many now-established, invasive plants, we'll probably never get rid of garlic mustard. That's all the more reason to use it as much as possible. So pick and use all you want, since you needn't worry about exhausting the supply. And if you have any lingering doubt as to whether or not the plant at hand is garlic mustard, just pick some and crush it. The powerful garlic aroma will quickly dispel any doubts.

Common Blue Violet

Fair, dainty beauty, scorned and trampled underfoot. Common blue violets deserve better than to be walked on and then mowed down in the prime of life. That explains why I always wait until the last possible moment to mow my lawn for the first time each year. It seems such a shame to destroy the deep blue swath of color provided by the wild violets that inhabit my lawn. Once gone, they remain gone, not to return for another year. The plants grow new leaves, though, so all is not lost.

Scarce a soul who has ever walked along a rural lane or stepped along the edge of a lawn in spring does not recognize our common blue violet, *Viola pa-*

pilionacea, on sight. The roughly-toothed, heart-shaped leaves and five-petaled flowers grow on single stalks. The naked flowerstalk rises only a slight bit above the leaves.

Common blue violets mark a transition time in Maine, a season when early spring plants have gone past their prime and summer plants have not yet begun to show. It is late spring, but hard frosts are still a possibility. Summer, though, looms just over the horizon.

But back to that inevitable chore, the first lawn mowing of the season. Knowing that my violets are doomed, I do my best to honor their beauty. A week or so before mowing, I begin picking blossoms, putting a single violet blossom in each compartment of an ice cube tray and freezing them as such, an attractive complement to cold summer drinks. Also, on my way to check my mailbox, I always stop and pick a handful of violet blossoms as a trail nibble. I find them to have a sweet, slightly nutty flavor. And each day, a small glass, half-filled with spring water and stuffed full of violet blossoms, graces my kitchen table.

Even before violets go into full bloom, I began my harvest by picking the leaves and using them as a potherb, boiling until they are fork tender. Although the taste of these, when drained and served with butter, pleases me, I cannot find a suitable way to describe it. So try a small helping first. Chances are, you will not only like it, but also like it a lot. If that's the case, then know that every time you eat a side of cooked violet leaves, you are getting a whopping dose of vitamin C. By now, though, it shouldn't come as a surprise that these wild edibles abound in useful vitamins.

Violet syrup, a pleasant and versatile product, is easy to make. Just fill any size glass jar with violet blossoms and cover with boiling, sugar water. Use one cup sugar to two cups water (for a thicker syrup, use up to two cups sugar to one cup water) and cover when the jar becomes cool to the touch. Allow to stand overnight. Then drain the liquid and discard the now white (it's fun to watch the blue color leach out of the violet blossoms while adding the boiling water) blossoms.

For a pretty raspberry color, add a squirt of lemon juice. The acid in the juice turns the syrup red.

Store the finished syrup in a cool, dark closet or in the refrigerator. I like it on pancakes and often choose it over maple syrup. Also, this syrup makes a fine, gentle medicine for a scratchy throat. At the first sign of sore throat or hoarseness, I like to let a tablespoon of violet syrup trickle down my throat. This provides immediate relief.

Fortunately for me, common blue violets persist well into early summer, along the shady, wooded trails that twine around my woodlot. So even after the great majority have fallen to the mower's wrath, a few dainty blue violets remain to cheer me on my way.

For those who absolutely love having violets around, know that they transplant well and appear to thrive in containers. I discovered this trait when violets kept popping up in my hanging flower baskets. Even after the cultivated flowers died, the uninvited violets remained healthy. So for violets even after the season has ended, try planting in containers. Also, most wild plants, when given rich soil and lots of close attention, grow unusually large. Perhaps common blue violets will become the next garden rage.

Groundnuts

Groundnuts, *Apios americana,* for many years remained an enigma for me. People told me of the potato-like tubers and of their fine table qualities. But nobody ever told me how to locate groundnuts, except to say that they grow along streams. What streams? Where, exactly? All I ever got were vague descriptions of where to find groundnuts.

Without a doubt, my youthful wanderings took me past untold pounds of this delicious root crop. But not recognizing them for what they were, I passed by without a second glance. Then one day, while trout fishing in early spring, around coltsfoot time, I saw a rather odd root strung out on the bank of a slow-moving stream. This string-like root connected numerous potato-like tubers, strung out along its length. Immediately, I knelt down to examine this curious find and exclaimed, to no one in particular, "Groundnuts."

Groundnut tubers range in size: shown here the size of cherry tomatoes.

Find strings of groundnut tubers in early spring along streams and rivers.

After that, I began locating groundnuts nearly everywhere. In time, it became apparent that it wasn't always necessary to find the tubers exposed, on top of the ground, but only to find the pea-like vines. Then, some manual work with a spade or garden trowel would reveal the hidden treasure.

So to what cause might we attribute the tubers being laid out in the open, there for the taking? In most cases, high water and accompanying ice floes of late winter and spring dislodge the tubers, sweeping them downstream. As water levels recede, the strings of groundnuts lay where they dropped. In time, these would no doubt take root and establish a new groundnut colony. Groundnuts are terribly aggressive, more so than the unjustly hated, Japanese knotweed. But when strings of groundnuts present themselves to opportunistic fishermen/foragers, it prevents the establishment of a new colony.

It makes me smile to recollect the many times a fellow angler has asked if I had taken any trout. As a rule, I unceremoniously pop groundnuts into my creel, along with any fish. So upon opening the lid, the viewer sees not only whatever trout might reside therein, but also fresh-picked groundnuts.

When this happens, after explaining the nature of the plant, I often present a handful of tubers as a gift, hoping to convert yet another person to the pleasures of harvesting and eating groundnuts.

While groundnuts aren't nuts at all, their common name describes their appearance and habits fairly well. They are about the size of a large walnut and, of course, they live underground. Here again, I rarely set out, spade in hand, to dig a mess of groundnuts. Instead, nature offers enough of the loose, above-ground variety to serve my needs and quench my appetite for these sweet tubers.

Anyone seeing the tubers for the first time should immediately recognize them as groundnuts. Some of them are considerably larger than walnuts, some smaller. But all are covered with a mesh-like fiber, rather like the hairy fiber covering on a coconut. The vines, which have in past years been likened to wisteria they closely resemble, do not stand by themselves, but instead rely upon other plants for support. So closely and thickly do these vines grow that they have actually strangled and killed young Japanese knotweed plants.

The leaves are divided into five to seven sharply pointed, toothless leaflets. The light-brown blossoms, which closely resemble pea blossoms, grow from the leaf axles (the vertex of the joint formed by plant stem and leaf stem) and have a remarkably sweet aroma. In fact, this near-cloying scent reaches out for a great distance, helping lead foragers to the plant.

To prepare, peel your groundnuts. A slotted vegetable peeler helps tremendously, allowing you to peel even fairly small groundnuts. Then, just boil in water as per potatoes. Serve piping hot with butter, salt and pepper. Eat while still warm, since they lose flavor after cooling.

Groundnuts certainly don't take the place of potatoes or other root crops in my diet. Instead, they supplement them. And while groundnuts can be dug and eaten most any time conditions permit, I prefer to revel in them in season, when they present themselves to me as I walk the rivers, streams and brooks of Maine.

Partridgeberries are the perfect trail nibble.

Partridgeberry

Probably more people recognize this diminutive woodland plant as an essential terrarium component than as a wild food. But such as they are, partridgeberries, *Mitchella repens*, make a moderately good trail nibble. These have such a mild flavor as to make them uninspiring. Also, the berries contain quite a few small seeds. But their pretty red color and ready availability make them of value despite their few drawbacks.

Look for these ground-hugging vines, or stems, in the dappled shade of both deciduous and coniferous woodlands. The roundish leaves have a prominent, light-colored midrib, with a small number of obvious veins extending from that. Also, the leaves are paired, growing opposite each other on the stem. The delicate white and pink flowers appear in pairs at the end of each vine, or stem. These combine to produce one red berry.

The main value of partridgeberry, then, lies in its attractive structure and in the beauty of its berries. Besides, anything that can be picked and eaten out-of-hand has worth. So while hiking, fishing or just plain walking in the woods, look for partridgeberries and try nibbling on them.

Wild Sarsaparilla

If all the wild sarsaparilla in Maine were dug and the roots laid out in a straight line, how far would that line extend? To the moon, perhaps? Of course this is a question without an answer. But it serves to illustrate my point that wild sarsaparilla, *Aralia nudicaulis,* grows rampantly in our humus-rich, somewhat acid, woodland soil. A vast network of roots extends horizontally, just inches below the surface.

These roots were once widely dug, hearkening back to when they were the basis for a popular drink. Also, wild sarsaparilla was (and still is, by herbalists) considered a tonic and blood purifier. Now, not only does sarsaparilla go pretty much unnoticed, it even gets confused with toxic plants.

I've heard of people referring to wild sarsaparilla as "poison mercury," a folk name for the toxic *Mercurialis perennis*, also known as dog mercury. Also, wild sarsaparilla bears more than a passing resemblance to immature poison ivy. When young, sarsaparilla leaves exhibit a shiny, reddish tint, somewhat akin to poison ivy. Closer examination of suspect plants should prove the difference, though.

Poison ivy has leaves in groups of three. Sarsaparilla has a twice-divided, five-parted leaf, with three leaf blades or leaflets on the end and a gap separating these from the lower two. Sarsaparilla leaves are quite finely toothed, while poison ivy has only a few, irregular indentations. Finally, poison ivy has erect vines

In spring wild sarsaparilla (inset) resembles toxic poison ivy, but in summer any similarity ends.

that often climb trees and rocks, whereas wild sarsaparilla has only a leafstalk and, later, a flowerstalk.

As wild sarsaparilla matures, the leaves lose all traces of red and also lose their shiny tint, it being replaced by a flat green hue.

In late spring, wild sarsaparilla makes an attractive groundcover in shady woodlands. Then, with all traces of resemblance to poison ivy gone, foragers can harvest the roots for the making of a pleasant tea. Just grab the crown and gently pull. In the loose soil that sarsaparilla prefers, the roots should easily pop out of the ground. Use constant, steady tension in order to loosen the longest possible root section.

Then, back home, peel the roots. I use a jackknife, since the brown outer covering peels easily. A vegetable peeler works, too. After peeling, notice how white and smooth the roots appear. Also, notice the pronounced sarsaparilla scent. Chop two teaspoons of root, more for a stronger beverage, and place in a teacup. Cover with boiling water and steep. The roots should sink to the bottom. You might prefer to strain before drinking, though. I like this tea just as is, but a little honey or sugar won't hurt, either.

Wild sarsaparilla provides a soothing drink, one that most likely includes a few health benefits as well.

Summer

Summer in Maine brings a host of new and different useful wild plants. Often, these grow in unlikely places, including our flower and vegetable gardens and also along the seashore. This brief stretch of sun-splashed, warm days has much to recommend it, as evidenced by the huge number of tourists and sightseers who trek to Maine each summer. For me, though, the great number of wild edible plants marks the best part of this glorious season.

Wild Mint

To put myself in a proper frame of mind for writing this chapter, I brewed a cup of wild mint tea. It sits, steeping, on my writing desk. A powerful mint aroma wafts upward, pleasing to my senses and reminding me just how worthwhile it was when, last summer, I walked along a local river and harvested a great quantity of this native mint.

An antique silver tea ball, one of the few items of silver tableware passed down from my ancestors, holds something less than one, rounded teaspoon. And that's all it takes to make a heady cup of hot mint tea.

Our native mint, wild mint, *Mentha arvensis*, was utilized by Native Americans long before European colonization. But with the colonists came their mints and some of these have become naturalized. Among these are spearmint, *Mentha spicata* and water mint, *Mentha aquatica*.

For a brief list of Old World mints, I will quote from *Anne Pratt's Flowering Plants of Great Britain, 1870*: "It is not unlikely that in former days more species were in common culture in this country, where now the Spearmint and Peppermint are the two plants chiefly selected. Our fathers had also their Crosse Mint, Browne Mint, Mackerel Mint, Curled Mint, Holy Blackfish Mint, Heart Mint, Fish Mint and Brook Mint."

Of course we can only wonder about the taste of any mint bearing the curious name of "Holy Blackfish Mint." The nature of mints featuring these common names are, to my knowledge, lost in the dim mists of history. Still, such an extensive list does much to inform modern readers of the importance that the British attached to mints over 140 years ago.

But for zing, pungency, strength and also medicinal properties, nothing beats our own native wild mint.

Wild mint grows along streams, brooks, rivers, lakes and ponds. Often, the plants become inundated during times of high water. This appears to harm them not in the least and may, in fact, be beneficial.

Wild mint has a square stem, with blossoms in the leaf axils.

All the mints have square stems, wild mint included. The egg-shaped leaves grow opposite each other up and down the long, spindly stem. Flowers, tiny and bell-shaped, grow in whorls in the leaf axils (between leaf and stem). These are at different times and different locations, white, lavender or a light shade of violet.

The plant has a sprawling style, and seldom attains more than one foot or a bit more before falling back and spreading out. Wild mint is oftentimes fuzzy, or hairy and as often as not, quite smooth. In other words, this species has many variable aspects. I find identification complete only when, after crushing a quantity in my hand, it exudes its strong, mint flavor.

Taste being subjective, it warrants pointing out that mints all have similar uses and if someone prefers peppermint, spearmint or water mint, what of it? We all have our likes and dislikes. As for me, I like wild mint.

Every year in late summer, when the water in local streams has receded so as to permit walking up and down along the rocky shoreline with something like relative ease, I go on a wild mint foraging expedition. Interestingly, while having never found wild mint that I didn't like, some locations yield better-tasting, more fragrant mint than others. Consequently, I have my favorite wild mint streams.

Since this mint has such shallow roots, care must be taken to make sure we don't pull the entire plant. For that reason, I like to grab a big handful with one hand and with a pocketknife held in the other hand, sever the stems. This results in one big bunch of mint. It doesn't take long to harvest a large quantity of mint. But in this case, more, rather than less, makes great sense.

While fresh mint works fine for teas and also for flavoring meat and fish, it is the dried mint that we rely upon for year-round use. So after returning home with my wild mint, I spread it out on a table and check for sticks, leaves and other plants that may have come along for the ride. Then, I place my mint in a colander and rinse it thoroughly. This is more to wash away any water-borne pollutants that might be present than to rid the mint of any sticks and so on that I may have missed.

Next, the mint is placed in a large basket and suspended in a cool, airy, shady location to thoroughly dry. After drying, which may take three or more days, depending upon the relative humidity, the mint is ready for processing.

To process your dry mint, just roll between your fingers, crushing the leaves and separating the stems. Remove and discard all woody matter and thicker parts of stems. Then, place the crushed, dried mint in an airtight container and store in a cool closet.

Uses of wild mint are legion. My favorite culinary uses include applying it as a rub on lamb roasts and also, sprinkling in the body cavity of salmon and large trout prior to broiling. And, of course, a cup of hot mint tea, sans sugar, lemon or any other additions, is my favorite use of all. This tea also tastes good when chilled and served as ice tea.

Wild mint grows along and sometimes in, streams and brooks.

World literature abounds in references to mint. It was included in the tithes required of the ancient Hebrews. Also, Chaucer, in his, *"Romaunt of the Rose,"* wrote:

> *"Then went I forthe on my right honde,*
> *Downe by a little path I fonde*
> *Of mintes full and fenell greene."*

As a youngster, my grandma gave me mint tea for a bellyache or when I just plain didn't feel well. This usually had a salutary effect upon my real or imagined ills.

One thing is for sure regarding wild mint's medicinal uses. Whatever the problem, it might help and surely won't hurt.

Wild Horseradish

Much of Maine was once farm country. But now, most of the farms are gone, and working fields have made the transition to woodlands. Still, the cellar holes remain. Often, offspring of once-cultivated plants remain. Asparagus, having self-seeded, persists on the old farm places, as does Japanese knotweed, planted as an ornamental, along with various perennial flowers and shrubs.

Another hanger-on from days gone by, horseradish, *Armoracia rusticana*, is one of the first wild plants I look for when inspecting a newfound cellar hole. The leaves, most of which grow directly from the root crown or top, are long and wavy on the edges and coarsely toothed. For a comparison, horseradish leaves somewhat resemble the leaves of curled dock. When in bloom, horseradish displays lots of small, white, four-petaled flowers. These grow on long, many-branched stems, or panicles. The four-petaled, or cross-shaped flowers confirm horseradish's place in the mustard family.

As with many other escapees from cultivation, "wild" horseradish is nothing but regular, cultivated horseradish that has escaped cultivation and persists in the wild. The wild variety isn't any better than the tame kind, but for those who don't grow horseradish, the wild plant stands as a good substitute. Besides that it's free, and the places where it is found are almost always scenic or attractive, pleasant spots to visit.

Wild horseradish has many uses, the most common being ground fine and mixed with white vinegar to make a pungent condiment. Just grind (I sometimes use a kitchen grater instead of a grinder) and add vinegar until the mixture resembles a paste. Stored in the refrigerator, it will remain good to go for many months.

The young leaves offer another taste treat. These are among the tastiest and most nourishing early greens out there. My introduction to horseradish leaves came when an old-timer told me how when he was young; his mother would

The most common usage of horseradish is finely grinding or chopping the roots and mixing with white vinegar to make a pungent condiment

gather a big batch of horseradish leaves and cook them up for the family. This meal was a rite of spring, and while they probably didn't realize it, they were getting a mega-dose of healthful vitamins and minerals, something much-needed after a winter of subsiding on canned, smoked and salted food.

As it turned out, I had a patch of horseradish in my garden and was able to give my friend a heaping armload. His story inspired me to try the greens myself, and after briefly steaming them, I had them with just a touch of apple cider vinegar and found them delicious. And knowing that the greens were rich in Vitamins A and C, along with other trace nutrients common to mustards, made the meal even more satisfying.

Ground horseradish root figures prominently in folk medicine and its uses are legion. But suffice it to say, I feel the best way to use it is a food. Adding horseradish sauce to any dish amounts to adding very tasty but effective medicine.

It's a wonder that the pharmaceutical industry hasn't recognized the value of horseradish as a healer and compounded some form of it to be sold at extraordinary prices. But since patents are not available for wild plants, there is no money in it. Thankfully, we can't buy horseradish pills, which means we must go afield and harvest our own and take it home and process it. And that, in my mind, stands at the apex of sensible living, combining healthy exercise in the outdoors with harvesting a tasty and healthful plant.

Dame's Rocket

This ultra-fragrant wildflower gets part of its name from its habit of being sweetest in the evening. Indeed, *Hesperis matronalis,* dame's rocket, gets its botanical name from *hespros,* meaning, "the evening."

Casual observers may quite naturally assume that dame's rocket is some form of wild garden phlox. The two certainly share a similar appearance. But phlox flowers have five petals and rocket has only four. In fact, rocket is a crucifer, a member of the mustard family. And any mention of the mustards must immediately elicit thoughts of edibility.

Much to the cottage gardener's delight, this self-seeding, hairy-stemmed biennial grows to a height of two or three feet, making it a perfect foil for the back of a perennial bed. The fragrant, four-petaled flowers appear in groups atop the stem. The finely toothed leaves are generally elliptical and broad at the base. Flowers appear in pink, purple or white. Dame's rocket, a native of Europe, has become firmly naturalized throughout Maine.

In what I deem a misguided decision, Maine has included Dame's Rocket in its list of invasive plants. It is not invasive and does not displace native plants.

Being a biennial, dame's rocket self-seeds readily. These seeds, when landing on disturbed or cultivated ground, will germinate and produce new plants.

Young Dame's Rocket leaves make a tasty potherb.

The flowers of Dame's Rocket emit a sweet perfume.

And that is precisely how dame's rocket became so prevalent on my woodland yard. I scattered seed in front of my cottage on the open, south-facing side. And now, beginning in June and lasting throughout the summer, I have colorful, fragrant and also edible, dame's rocket to cheer me.

It is the leaves that we use from dame's rocket, as potherbs. These require cooking for perhaps three or four minutes in boiling water before being drained and served up, piping hot. The taste is reminiscent of lamb's quarters and also, radish tops, but milder than the latter.

As an aside, I have trouble growing radishes. The roots quickly become hot and woody. Also, insects attack them with a vengeance. But it is not for the root that I grow them but rather, for the leaves. These make a fairly strong, but tasty potherb. And since both rocket and radishes are crucifers, my comparison to dame's rocket leaves seems justified.

Dame's rocket was once greatly appreciated as an ornamental and a few people still utilize it in yard and garden designs. In fact, a dense grouping of dame's rocket makes a striking sight in early summer.

Dame's rocket grows in the open, where it gets plenty of sunlight. This includes along the south-facing side of hedgerows, fallow fields, along garden edges and even in the bony, gravelly soil of railroad right-of-ways. Once established it is easy to maintain, since it requires no maintenance.

Often, people ask me if I eat flowers. This is usually asked with a tint of sarcasm. But I always smile and answer, "Yes...dame's rocket. And it is delicious."

Pickerelweed

Despite a lifelong acquaintance with pickerelweed, *Pontederia cordata*, I have never eaten the leaves. Various field guides to wild plants mention that these, when picked young, before they completely unfurl, make a fine salad addition as well as a cooked green.

Why this gap in my life list of wild edibles either eaten or at least sampled? Well, it has to do with my absolute love for fishing. Pickerelweed grows in shallow areas of lakes and ponds, as well as along the shore of slow-moving streams and thoroughfares. It requires a boat or canoe to gain access to pickerelweed and quite simply put, when I am in a boat in springtime when pickerelweed is ripe, my mind is set on fishing and nothing else.

Pickerelweed leaves are dark green, with a prominent midrib and less prominent venation to either side of that. Roundly pointed at the end and cleft at the bottom, in a sort of "folk-heart" shape, pickerelweed is easily identified.

Someday I plan to take time from fishing and gather a basket of pickerelweed leaves to take home and try. But, of course, that all depends upon how the fish are biting. Others, however, might make it a point to try these abundant, widely-available greens as soon as possible. If you do, please let me know how you like them.

Pickerelweed grows in most shallow lakes, ponds and streams in Maine. It appears in large colonies.

But fall is another matter entirely. Now, fish don't bite quite as well as in spring, leaving latter-day Isaac Waltons such as me with more free time. And that's when I make it a point to gather fruiting seed spikes of pickerelweed. This requires, in addition to some kind of watercraft, a basket and a jackknife.

Cut the spike just under the flowering head and drop in the basket. While you're out there, it just makes sense to pick a good supply. Upon returning home, spread the spikes loosely on a screen, in a large basket or even in a dark, cool closet. Allow them to dry and then rub whatever little blue bits of flower remain. After that, pick out each little segment on the spike. These are the nutlets and they remind me of sunflower seeds.

Of course you can sample the fresh nutlets as soon as you get home. They make a fine treat when eaten out-of-hand. I prefer to dry them and use as snacks and they make a refreshing, delicious, pick-me-up. You might want to add a bit of fine-ground sea salt, but that's not necessary. The dried nutlets taste plenty good on their own.

An enterprising forager might consider using dried pickerelweed nutlets as a form of breakfast cereal or perhaps as the main ingredient in a granola mixture. Your imagination is the only limiting factor here.

As with so many other excellent wild, edible plants, pickerelweed is abundant enough to support legions of foragers without any fear of depleting the resource. But that probably won't happen, given that it requires a watercraft to get to prime pickerelweed spots.

And so pickerelweed will continue growing as it has for millennia, without much interference from humans one way or the other.

Comfrey

Comfrey, *Symphytum officinale,* also goes by the common name of knitbone. An alien, no doubt purposely transported here from Europe because of its curative powers, comfrey has naturalized and now grows in scattered locations throughout Maine.

To call comfrey "tenacious" is a gross understatement. When left undisturbed, comfrey spreads quite slowly. But trying to remove comfrey by digging is to awaken, and even aggravate, a sleeping giant. Sure, comfrey transplants easily. But all our efforts, no matter how intense, are insufficient to completely eradicate the plant once firmly established. In other words, transplanting comfrey means that not only will the plant have a new location, it will still thrive in the old location.

A friend once decided to expand his lawn. To that end, he hired a dozer to come in and do the work. He failed to calculate the end result of bulldozing the several dozen comfrey plants that his father had planted for food and medicine,

Comfrey is an invasive garden plant that has escaped into the wild.

many years before. The dozer did a fine job of evenly distributing comfrey over approximately a full acre.

For those who admire this coarse, aggressive plant, it makes sense to confine comfrey to containers and not to permit it to gain a foothold in the ground.

When traveling around Maine's back roads and rural areas, it is common to see comfrey growing far from any habitation. But stop, get out and look around and it's a sure bet that an old cellar hole or foundation is close by. Comfrey was once a staple, kept mostly for its medical uses.

Studies indicate that internal use of comfrey is potentially hazardous. That's a shame, since the young leaves make a fine potherb. I sometimes eat a mess of immature comfrey greens and am convinced that breathing polluted air or eating chemically-laden, commercially-raised foods poses a far greater health risk. But in this case, please do as I say and not as I do. Comfrey poses no threat when used externally, a good thing because it is an effective healer.

Both the roots and leaves are made into a healing poultice for bruises, strains, sprains and, in days past, broken bones. To make a poultice, chop or grind (a blender or food chopper works well for this) the plant so that it turns into a kind of paste. If needed, add a bit of cooking oil to moisten the paste. Place the poultice over the problem area and cover with a cloth so as to hold it in place.

I have used comfrey for bruises and also cuts that were slow to heal. It works very well for these external applications.

Comfrey has long, hairy leaves that are usually erect, except after a heavy rain, when they flatten out and fall to the ground. Oddly, the leaves rarely stand aright again and the plant quickly pushes up new leaves to take their place. Also, the leaves exhibit a mosaic-type of venation. The flowers are round and tubular. It would be a stretch to call them bell-shaped, though. Comfrey flowers are usually a light blue, but they can appear in shades of purple, pink and even white.

It might be best to find comfrey growing in the wild and harvest it as needed, rather than growing it at home. But either way, comfrey has a definite use as a healing plant.

Common Milkweed

Common milkweed, *Asclepias syriaca,* hardly needs describing. And yet, two toxic plants may, conceivably, be mistaken for milkweed. These are dogbane and butterfly weed, or pleurisy root. Dogbane, *Apocynum* species, has a much more slender stem and long, paired seedpods. In general, it is a frail plant when compared to common milkweed. Butterfly weed, *Asclepias tuberosa*, lacks the white latex sap of common milkweed. Also, butterfly weed has bright-orange flowers and the seedpods are far more slender than those of common milkweed.

That said, every child recognizes common milkweed by its warty, pointed seedpods, the fluffy-white parachutes that bear the seeds so far on even the most gentle breeze, and the sticky white sap. My memory takes me back to the time when, as a very young boy, I tried licking the sticky "milk." It was bitter and

Tips and buds are edible parts of common milkweed.

The young, tender pods of the common milkweed are edible.

had a terrible taste, a taste that lingered far too long in my mouth. Fortunately, cooking totally removes any unpleasant taste.

Common milkweed provides three different food products, and the first one is ready in early summer, as soon as the young plant becomes visible on lawns, fields and along roadsides.

When viewed from directly above, common milkweed leaves are in upright pairs, with each pair rotated one half turn from the other. The terminal, or end tips, with their four small leaves, make the first milkweed product of the year. Just pinch these off, using thumb and forefinger. Remember, though, that even these tip-top leaves exude that sticky white latex, so make sure not to use your best or most precious container.

It takes only a short while to pick a pint or so of these, especially when working with a large stand of common milkweed. Treat these young leaves as you would green beans. That is, boil them until they become fork-tender. This may take up to ten minutes. Keep checking them, and when done, they become quite limp. Strain and serve with salt, pepper and butter.

It might seem that picking all the terminal leaves from a stand of common milkweed would set the plants back. But in my experience, that just doesn't happen. By season's end, it is difficult to locate plants that have had their leaves harvested. So pick away, especially if you find this free wild product to your liking.

By late June or early July, common milkweed produces a huge flush of broccoli-like buds. The young buds are light green and only about the size of a large marble. Again, harvesting these small buds does not seem harmful to the plant.

Common Milkweed provides three different food products. The dried seedpods are often used in dried flower arrangements.

Just wait a few weeks and return to the same stand of milkweed. It will appear as if you either missed picking a substantial number of buds, or that the plant has produced a new flush of them. The latter answer seems more reasonable.

Anyway, since the buds sit atop a stem, they, like the leaves, exude the same milky latex. For that reason, I use an old basket that has seen better days. Also, if the latex gets on your hands, it becomes something like a kind of glue. Wearing disposable gloves to pick common milkweed solves this problem. Since I find milkweed only a short distance down the road from my house, I dispense with the gloves and wash my hands with warm soapy water back at home. However you choose to deal with it, though, remember that picking common milkweed products is somewhat messy.

Cook the buds as per broccoli, by first boiling a slight amount of water in a saucepan and then dropping the buds in. Let them cook at a low boil until they acquire a light green color. Drain and serve with the usual complement of butter and spices. These buds are my favorite milkweed product and rival any cultivated vegetable in texture, attractiveness and taste.

In time, the flower buds become less compact and also take on a reddish tint. They remain fine for eating, as long as the flowers haven't yet opened. Texture is the only difference between these adult buds and the younger ones. Young buds are dense, compact and older ones are only loosely arranged.

As many buds as I pick from the relatively small stand of common milkweed near my place, the plants always manage to produce their signature seedpods. These are between one and three inches long, tapered at the end and warty. Later on, the pods open and the seeds disperse to the prevailing wind, carried on their white, fluffy parachutes. But as long as the pods remain soft and flexible, they are good for eating.

Pick as many as you wish, remembering that these, too, exude their sticky sap. Cook them by boiling for at least ten minutes. Longer cooking won't hurt the product. Interestingly, cooking turns the white fluff inside the pods to a delicious, starchy product. Common milkweed pods may rate as one of the more interesting wild plant foods.

The cooked pods are so tasty that I like to blanch and freeze a few bags for winter use. When January winds blow and temperatures plummet, having a plate of common milkweed pods from the previous summer seems a great way to defy the elements.

Cattail Stalks, Flower Spikes, Pollen

Now, in summer, common cattails, *Typha latifolia*, sway three or four feet above the water. The first prize of summer is the young shoots. These form in layers, in a way similar to leeks. A cross-section of one reveals something like the annular rings on a tree. Cut them near the water's surface and trim and retain the bottom six or eight inches, that being the tenderest. Peel away the outer layer or two, and inside find a clean white vegetable, suitable for a variety of uses.

Eat cattail flower spikes as corn-on-the-cob with a little butter, salt and pepper.

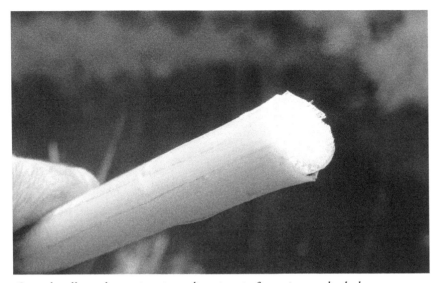

Cattail stalks make a prime ingredient in stir-fry recipes and salads.

The first use, and one of my favorites, is as a trail nibble. But human foragers aren't the only ones to appreciate young cattail stalks. Muskrats nibble on them as well, leaving evidence of their feast scattered about the shore of ponds and slow-moving streams.

Here again, I must suggest that foragers not follow my lead in picking and eating cattail stalks out-of-hand. Pollutants in the water may adhere to the stalks, even though they are peeled and the outside covering discarded. So for safety sake, take them home and rinse in clean water before eating.

A large stand of cattails yields far more than anyone could ever eat at one sitting. Harvesting has no noticeable effect on the plants either. Just ask any pond owner who has tried every imaginable device to rid a farm pond of cattails.

So pick as many as you want, using a sharp jackknife to sever the stalks. Place them in a basket and take them home for further use. Peel and rinse and then place the tender stalks on a cutting board and chop into half-inch sections. While these make a fine contribution to any salad, they truly excel as a main ingredient in stir-fry recipes. Just don't overcook. After all, the stalks are tender to begin with.

The 4th of July sees most Mainers attending cookouts, going to lakeside camps and enjoying firework displays. My favorite 4th of July tradition involves visiting a local wetland. By then, cattail spikes have ripened to a point where they are suitable for harvesting.

The immature flower spikes grow atop the larger, brown spikes. These are partially covered by a thin sheath, from which they are easily removed. To test these spikes for readiness, just take a thumbnail and prod the spike. The grainy "meat" of the spike should crumble under just slight pressure. If this doesn't happen, wait a few days and try again.

Collect as many of these spikes as you can haul and take them home to prepare. These can sit in a refrigerator for several days without any noticeable change in texture or flavor. To cook, treat the spikes the same as corn-on-the-cob. Bring water in a large saucepan to a rolling boil and drop in as many cattail spikes as you might wish to eat. Cook for approximately five minutes and drain. Use plenty of butter, the same as you would with corn, and eat the spikes in a similar way. Fortunately, the inner core, or stiff part of the stalk makes a useful, ersatz, "handle."

I like these so well that I try and freeze at least a few packages each year. Just blanch for a few minutes, place in ice water to cool, drain and throw in a freezer bag.

Never has a single guest to my home ever declined a second helping of cooked cattail spikes. That speaks volumes about their high quality.

My final trip to the wetlands where the common cattails grow happens a week or so after the last spike harvest. Then, the spikes acquire a coating of bright-yellow pollen. Over time, people have put cattail pollen to several different uses. An ancient plant book in my library says, "Gerarde records *that downe of the reed-mace hath been proved to heale kibbed or humbled heels.*"

That same book mentions that the pollen, being extremely flammable, was used in fireworks exhibitions. It's far more likely that pollen from running clubmoss, *Lycopodium clavatum*, which is also yellow and very flammable, was used in fireworks rather than cattail pollen. And as far as healing humbled heels, I would probably first turn to talcum powder if I felt that my heels had been humbled.

But cattail pollen does, indeed, have a perfectly fine use in the kitchen. It works wonderfully when mixed, half and half, with wheat or other flour. The cattail pollen not only adds a pleasing color, but also a pleasant flavor. I enjoy it in pancakes, especially pancakes to which dried elderberries were added to the batter. But more on them later. For now, collect cattail pollen by holding the pollen-coated spike over a paper bag and tapping. A huge plume of smoky pollen will fall into the bag. A dedicated harvester can easily gather a quart or so in five minutes' time.

Back home, it pays to spread the pollen out on a large sheet of paper in order to check for any insects that might have attached themselves to the flower spike. Store the pollen in a tightly-closed glass vessel and use as needed.

It's for sure that we can't live on cattails alone, but if push came to shove, the common cattail could certainly sustain us until better times prevailed.

Common Plantain

I like to point out that everyone, no matter where they live, has access to edible wild plants. And common plantain, *Plantago major*, always backs up my statement. It grows practically everywhere on cleared ground. This includes ball fields, lawns and even vacant lots in major metropolitan areas.

The broad green leaves, with their prominent veins, are easily recognized. To further assist in identification, the seed stems surmount the leaves by several inches. Finally, most children know how to "shoot" the seeds from common plantain spikes by sliding clenched thumb and forefinger the length of the stalk. This plant is known to all who wander the forest and fields of Maine. In fact, it is another of those naturalized plants, having found its way to the new world in fodder brought over by early colonists.

Common plantain has a couple of different uses. While I personally don't use it this way, the very young leaves can be added to salads. Its other use, that being as a cooked green, suits me better. Here again, use only young leaves, since older ones become too stringy (thanks to those prominent veins mentioned earlier) for table use. Cook in a slight amount of boiling water for only a few minutes, drain and serve. Treat cooked common plantain as you would spinach.

Plantains continue pushing up new leaves throughout the season, making it one of the few wild plants with an open-ended window of opportunity.

Admittedly, picking only the tender young leaves is tedious. On the other

Common plantain, potherb and medicinal plant.

hand it takes far less time to pick a meal's worth of common plantain than it does to jump in the car, drive to the store, buy vegetables and return home.

Finally, common plantain has great healing power. The crushed leaves are useful in healing sores and abrasions. Some people just chew the leaf and then place it on their hurt area. I prefer to chop my plantain with a knife or, better yet, to process it in a food chopper or blender. After placing the resulting paste on the area needing healing, bind it with some sterile gauze.

I have heard first-hand testimony of amazing results obtained from using common plantain in this manner. Plantain's medicinal use goes back many centuries. Shakespeare's Romeo said, regarding an injured shin, "Your plantain leaf is excellent for that." And Shenstone wrote:

> And pungent radish, biting infant's tongue,
> And plantain ribb'd, that heals the reaper's wound.

Indian Cucumber

Whoever gave this delicate woodland plant the common name of Indian cucumber should be forced to eat a bushel of those garden vegetables, skin and all, as penance. Indian cucumber, *Medeola virginiana*, bears absolutely no similarity to garden cucumbers, either in looks or taste. Anyone seeking a cucumber taste from wild plants should gather plenty of Clintonia, listed in the Spring chapter.

That said, the Indian cucumber root is sweet, mild and crunchy. It reminds me, at least in appearance and texture, of a white radish. Most people who have

The white edible root has a unique top growth punctuated by two leaf whorls.

tried it agree that Indian cucumber root is one of the better wild trail nibbles, perhaps even the best.

The above-ground section of this plant has a long glaucous (covered with white, lint-like fibers) stem and two whorls of sessile leaves. One of these whorls occurs about halfway up the stem. It has seven or eight leaves. The other whorl sits atop the steam and has three or four leaves. The flowers depend from the top as well. They are yellow, with reflexed, or bent tips and red stamens. The plant grows up to three feet tall, although most are closer to one foot or slightly more.

While Indian cucumber has an interesting above-ground structure, nothing about it suggests that it has a unique, tuber-like root. This grows horizontally, only an inch or so below the ground.

To locate a stand (don't pick unless you find a good-sized colony. If you find only one or two plants, it's best to leave them alone. They will spread and eventually form a larger group), walk along woodland edges, places where sunlight only dances on the forest floor. Indian cucumbers cannot survive for long in full sun or full shade.

After finding a sufficient number of adult plants to harvest, take pains to begin the process with great care. Simply pulling up the stem will result in the root top breaking, with nothing to show for your effort. Instead, with thumb and forefinger, dig down at the base of the stem and grasp the top of the root. Now, gently wiggle it but don't try pulling it up. As the root loses its grip on the forest humus, slowly work it out by pulling sideways.

To eat, just dust off any clinging loam, break off the few, stringy rootlets and enjoy. A finer snack does not exist anywhere in the Maine woods.

Valerian

Who would think, while driving along in July and seeing an endless swath of blooming white valerian, that this common roadside plant was an alien? Valerian, *Valeriana officinalis*, like so many other European arrivals, has done an admirable job of colonizing our state.

A medicinal plant, valerian also works well at the back of the perennial border. Its tall (to four feet) stature and primarily white flowerheads (a touch of pink is present, but it is very subdued) add a lovely touch to any garden. And come sundown, valerian releases a sweet, heady scent.

Valerian leaves are divided, with a feathery appearance. Only the lower leaves are toothed, and those quite coarsely.

If this doesn't serve to make an accurate identification, digging the spreading, thick root will. The root gives out a particular odor, one that I neither like nor dislike. Some people liken it to old sweat socks, but I consider that unfair. It does, though, remind me of an inexpensive brand of perfume.

Anyway, here is the catch. Valerian, like so many other medicinal plants, is

Valerian roots appear long and stringy. The flower clusters appear brilliant-white when viewed in bright sunshine.

most effective when harvested from poor ground. The beautiful plants that grow in nutrient-rich, garden soil are ineffectual, medicinally. But digging roots from the hard, gravelly ground where the most powerful plants grow is a difficult task.

Valerian is used in a decoction as a sedative. It works swiftly, unlike so many other plant remedies that have only a cumulative effect. To prepare for use, rinse all clinging dirt and gravel from the roots and allow to thoroughly dry. Then, with a sharp knife, chop the roots into small bits. Place two teaspoons (I personally use more, but to begin try and stick with the lower amount) in a cup or so of slowly-boiling water and allow to simmer for at least five minutes. Allow to cool and strain into a teacup or water glass. Drink all at once.

For some people, though, valerian has exactly the opposite effect. It acts as a stimulant. Oddly enough, a person who has had good results using valerian as a sedative might suddenly find that it no longer functions in that capacity. I know of no way to predict if and when the change will occur, either.

Those who buy medicinal herbs know that health-food stores abound in various brands of valerian products. These usually come in capsule form. It amazes me that people willingly pay significant sums of money to buy a processed plant, while the same thing grows all around and is not only free, but usually far more effective.

So for anyone who needs a little help relaxing or sleeping, valerian may be the answer. As with any medicinal product, always check with a physician before taking it.

Interestingly, in very late summer, all the tiny flowers fall from the flower-heads, but the "framework" remains. This skeletal form of the flowerhead acquires a pinkish-red hue and stands of valerian, when viewed from a distance, resemble a hazy-pink fog or shroud, hanging a few feet above the ground.

I can't leave this chapter on valerian without quoting Dodsley:

> *He the salubrious leaf*
> *Of cordial sage, the purple flowering head*
> *Of fragrant lavender, enlivening mint,*
> *Valerian's fetid smell, endows benign*
> *With their cephalic virtues.*

Heal-All

I have a hazy memory of being very sick as a young child and having my grandfather come to the rescue with a wild plant he called "bumblebee weed." Whatever it was that had me in its grip was debilitating. In addition to other symptoms, I had dysentery and the doctor's medicines did nothing to cure it.

I remember seeing a thick bunch of plants in grandpa's hand and also watching him instruct my mother in preparing the remedy. Under his tutelage, she got a large saucepan of water to boiling and then, after lightly chopping the whole plants, added them to the water. This simmered for the longest time and finally, she turned off the stove and removed the pan from the heat to allow it to cool.

The flower spike of heal-all appears somehow unfinished with only a few blooms open at once.

After that, it was up to me to drink a large water glass of the rather bitter dark-brown liquid. At that point, I would have taken anything, so I gathered my courage and downed the drink without protest. It worked, too. In fact, I later overheard the adults talking to each other about how the old man had probably saved my life with his plant remedy. Perhaps he had, too.

Heal-all, *Prunella vulgaris*, belongs in the mint family. As with so many other members of this large group, heal-all has a square stem, but lacks that familiar, minty aroma.

The plant, a perennial, seldom exceeds one foot in height. Leaves are opposite and lack teeth. The flowerspike resembles an old-time bee skep, thus grandpa's folk name, bumblebee weed. The lipped, dark-blue, sometimes tending toward pink, flowers never completely fill the spike, giving the impression that the thing is unfinished.

Introduced from Europe, heal-all was held in much esteem by British herbalists, who recommended its use for everything from mouth sores to cuts and bruises. Heal-all was reported seen growing in the Himalayas, which gives some idea of how far this low-growing plant ranges.

Look for heal-all in summer, blooming along field and road edges. Rarely does it grow in full sun, but it has taken hold in a few sunny sections of my lawn. There, it blooms when only a few inches tall, since it has no other choice. Mowing heal-all doesn't kill it, but only stunts the plants.

To make the above-mentioned liquid, just gather any amount of the plant and, after chopping or at least breaking it up, add stem, leaves and flowerspikes to boiling water. Simmer until the liquid has evaporated by half. Cool, drain through a colander and use as a rinse for mouth sores. Larger amounts do help with diarrhea, and the dose I use is a waterglass full every four hours.

Heal-all has definite astringent properties, which account for a number of its traditional uses. My personal regard for this unassuming plant has everything to do with that long-ago time when my grandpa came to my rescue with his wonderful wild plants.

Pineapple Weed

This low-growing annual is probably better known for what it isn't than for what it is. Pineapple weed, *Matricaria matricarioides,* so resembles chamomile that most casual observers take it for that plant, without question.

In Maine, most driveways and dooryard paths, at least unpaved ones, have a stand of pineapple weed growing alongside them. For the most part, these plants get walked on and driven on without regard to any potential usefulness.

Another alien, the question arises as to how pineapple weed arrived here in the first place. I'd like to think that people purposely saved seeds and later sowed them in the ground of the new world. But maybe the plant just arrived by accident. Either way, we'll never know for sure.

While pineapple weed has a few traditional medicinal uses attributed to it, my main use is as the main ingredient in a pleasant-tasting tea. In fact, when bruised or crushed, the blossom smells exactly like pineapple. Just as Clintonia smells exactly like cucumber, pineapple weed smells precisely like pineapple. And even in this day of synthetics and laboratory-produced, look-alikes and taste-alikes, I doubt that anyone could come closer to

Pineapple weed makes a pleasant-tasting tea.

true pineapple taste and aroma than nature has done with pineapple weed.

The leaves are finely dissected, so much so as to appear feathery. The flowers lack rays, or petals. The rounded, pale-yellow discs crumble easily with the slightest pressure from a thumb or finger. To harvest, pick only the blossoms. This is somewhat tedious, but it takes only a few teaspoons to make a delicious cup of tea.

Pineapple weed grows in full sun and also prefers the sterile, gravelly soil of driveway and lawn edges. Planting this in well-nourished garden soil would probably make for large, bushy plants with little active principal.

My fondness for this tea compels me to pick as much as possible and then dry it for winter use. A half-pint of dried discs is enough for many cups of tea.

When using fresh, add two heaping teaspoons to one cup boiling water. Dried product calls for only one teaspoon per cup of water. Some people prefer to drain their pineapple weed tea after it has steeped, but I'm content to stir it and allow the spent discs to sink to the bottom of my teacup.

One last note, don't harvest the discs from anywhere near where the exhaust of a motor vehicle blows on the ground. Otherwise, grab a kneeling pad and basket and have at the resident pineapple weed.

Queen Anne's Lace

Every kid from my era knew that the little red flower in the middle of a Queen Anne's Lace flowerhead represented a drop of blood from Queen Anne's finger, after she had pricked herself with a sewing needle. Somehow, I believe that that little red flower was present long before Queen Anne was even born.

Queen Anne's lace, *Daucus carota*, brings to mind the question of what came first, the carrot or Queen Anne's lace? They are alike, the only difference being that domestic carrots contain carotene (the ingredient that makes them orange) and Queen Anne's lace doesn't. Both have that familiar carrot taste.

What's more, if left to go wild, carrots revert back to Queen Anne's lace. And if Queen Anne's lace seeds are harvested, planted and saved over succeeding generations, the end product will become something like a regular garden carrot. Neat, huh?

Queen Anne's lace did not originate in America, and it is fascinating to speculate upon the possibility that it, in fact, sprung up from domestic carrots that had gone wild. But there is no way to know for sure. Either way, Queen Anne's lace has a long and reputable history of use in the old world, both as a prized root vegetable and also a medicinal herb.

I only use the plant as a food product, Queen Anne's lace not being among the small number of medicinal plants that I harvest each year for personal use. Also, I seldom eat the root, since it is so hard to find good ones in the compact clay that makes up my lawn. I do make the occasional effort to dig six or eight of the hardiest, straightest roots and cook and eat them, just to say that I did it. These are not as sweet as regular carrots, but as an emergency food, they are perfectly acceptable.

It has long been one of my goals to develop a typical-looking carrot from Queen Anne's lace. That would require saving seed from the best roots and planting and tending them through successive generations. Maybe I would call my carrot, QA1, for the first orange carrot developed from my experiments with Queen Anne's lace.

For me, a more regular use is in a tea. This use is one that I learned later in life, from my friend Suzie. Suzie said to use two whole flowerheads to a cup of boiling water. I later found that one flowerhead suffices to produce an aromatic, pleasant-tasting tea.

Others have written of the benefits of carrot seed tea, but Suzie's flowerhead tea is an entirely different product. It has much merit and I don't understand why it isn't more popular. Perhaps people just don't know about it.

Queen Anne's lace flower clusters make a distinctive tea.

The white root of Queen Anne's lace lacks the carotene that gives the domestic carrots their orange color.

Finally, for those who don't instantly recognize Queen Anne's lace, look for a two-to three-foot plant with a hairy stem and feathery, or lacy (thus the common name) leaves. Flowers blossom in flat-topped clusters. Later, when seeds develop, these clusters curl up and fold together, in the manner of a birdcage. Water hemlock, a toxic plant has leaves that are similar to Queen Anne's lace. However, water hemlock has hairless stalks. If you see something that resembles Queen Anne's lace but with a hairless stalk, don't touch it.

Sweetfern

Sweetfern, another plant with multiple uses, grows in poor soils near the coast of Maine and also inland, particularly on sandy soil. The scientific name, *Comptonia perigrina*, was named for Bishop Henry Compton, an early botanist.

My experience with sweetfern mostly encompasses those shrubs (sweetfern is a deciduous shrub) that grow within one hundred yards of the Penobscot Bay shoreline. But some years ago, when working in the White Mountains of New Hampshire, I was surprised to find plenty of sweetfern there as well. That seems reasonable though, since the soil there was poor and quite sandy. The plant also appears in some quantity in the sandy, mica-flecked soil of western Maine.

My personal favorite use of sweetfern is to simply break off a woody tip, crush the roundly-toothed, fernlike leaves and stick the whole thing in my shirt pocket. When hiking or fishing, the aromatic scent wafts past my nose, enhancing the total outdoor experience. If that were the only benefit we could reap from sweetfern, it would more than suffice. But the leaves have several other uses.

Sweetfern leaves make an outstanding herbal tea. Use standard measurements and allow to steep. Pleasant, aromatic, and to my way of thinking, relaxing, this tea stands as a fine example of the exquisite herbal teas available for free from the wild plants in Maine.

With such agreeable and inspiring tea ingredients available for free, it seems so needless for people to spend money on herbal teas offered in stores. For me, the knowledge that I picked the plant myself, coupled with the memory of a sun-filled day afield, makes Maine-grown wild teas infinitely more valuable than commercially-produced types. They are something to cherish.

But sweetfern has yet another property and this one may come as a surprise. The nuts—I like to refer to them as "nutlets," since they are so small—are tasty when eaten fresh, out-of-hand.

The nutlets are enclosed in a spiny, but not really prickly or dangerous to touch, burr. Each burr holds from one to four small nutlets. While I was aware of these tiny treats, it had never occurred to me to take time and try them. But one day on a plant walk with a friend and his five-year-old daughter, we stopped by a field filled with sweetfern and without hesitation, she began pulling the burrs apart and munching on the nutlets.

The seed-filled burrs (inset) of sweetfern look prickly but really are quite soft.

Sweetfern makes tasty tea and is an effective wash for poison ivy rash.

It all goes to show that we adults might benefit by paying more attention to the young. In this case, a plant-savvy five-year-old introduced me to a fine treat that I probably would never have tried without her intervention.

Sweetfern nutlets are far too small for harvesting and taking home. But if you can spare a few minutes while on a mid-to-late-summer walk here in Maine, do stop and try these excellent treats. A jackknife helps to open the burrs, but as my young friend illustrated, fingers work just fine. The nuts are generally round and whitish in color.

Finally, as with other wild plants found in Maine, sweetfern has not only a culinary but also a medical use. A strong tea, or even a decoction made by slowly simmering a large handful of leaves in a pint or so of water, makes a passable poison ivy remedy. This is to be applied at regular intervals, once the poison ivy rash has become evident.

I admit to never having used sweetfern tea as a wash for poison ivy because I have never had the need to. But others swear by its efficacy. In fact, one Maine farmer markets sweetfern leaves for the stated purpose of use as a wash for poison ivy rash.

Sweetfern also has a number of other (reputed) medicinal qualities in addition to its itch-relieving properties. I am content to use it as a pleasant air freshener, in a tea and if the need arises, as a wash for poison ivy rash.

Daylilies

Once, in a day when most Maine roads were dirt rather than asphalt, daylilies were ubiquitous along road margins. Even now, away from towns and cities, travelers on country roads thrill to seemingly endless rows of orange daylilies. And hikers, foragers, hunters and fishermen regularly encounter lush stands of daylilies around old cellar holes and crumbling foundations. These point out that our ancestors held daylilies in high enough regard to plant them around their yards.

Thinking about the life and times of our early settlers, it makes great sense that they would choose daylilies as one of their main ornamental plants. Once planted, daylilies require absolutely no attention. And in those days, people led physically-demanding lives and had little time for niceties. But the need for beauty couldn't be denied, so things such as daylilies and perhaps lilacs came to the rescue. By the way, daylilies are alien to this country and were purposely brought here from across the sea.

Unopened flower buds make a favorite cooked vegetable.

Daylilies grow to six feet tall. Their long, sword-shaped leaves grow thickly, closely packed. The flowerstalk is naked, or leafless and the orange flowers turn upward, as if purposely facing the sun. The flowers lack the black dots found on tiger lilies and Canada lilies.

Our common daylily, *Hemerocallis fulva*, gets its botanical name from *hemera*, which means a day and *kallos*, an indication of beauty. So the beautiful orange flowers last only one day. But the very next day, another takes its place. This process lasts for several weeks and it marks a high point of summer in Maine.

As with so many other useful wild plants, the daylily's beauty would be enough to endear it to us. But it has several culinary uses, making it a versatile plant, indeed.

To describe the various uses, I'll begin with the unopened flower buds, since they are my favorites. The tightly-closed buds appear in multiple numbers atop smooth, round stalks. Pick by snapping or trimming with a jackknife. Cook the same as per green beans, that is, by boiling until fork-tender. I like butter, salt and only a little pepper, since the cooked buds already exhibit a hint of peppery taste.

Here's an interesting anecdote. An attendee at a showing of my wild plant video shared this with me. He visited a friend, someone who raises a great variety of daylilies. Breeders have managed to establish hundreds of named and registered types of daylilies, many of them in exotic shapes and shades. These cultivated, hybridized lilies are a far cry from the common daylily seen along roadsides.

Anyway, the man told me that his friend introduced him to the joys of eating unopened daylily buds. He enjoyed them immensely and was pleased to learn that the wild/naturalized variety is edible as well. He also said, and this intrigued me greatly, that each variety of cultivated daylily has a slightly different taste.

Returning to our wild daylilies, the wilted blossoms make an interesting ingredient in stews and gumbos. In addition to their special taste, they act as a thickening agent. Freshly-wilted blossoms work well for this purpose and so do the dried variety. Just pick the spent blossoms, spread out on a nylon screen or loosely place on the bottom of a basket and allow to dry in a shady place with plenty of ventilation. Place the dried blossoms in a jar and use as needed.

The fresh as well as spent blossoms can be treated the same as squash blossoms. Roll in batter and deep-fry. Remove, drain on a paper towel and enjoy.

Finally, the tubers, shaped something like tiny sweet potatoes, are an excellent root crop. I don't bother peeling, but, rather, scrub them while holding under running water. Cook by boiling and serve with salt, pepper and butter. These have a pleasant, sweet flavor, not like a potato, but something all their own.

These tubers grow in great profusion and digging them doesn't harm the stand at all. In fact, digging here and there only thins the stand, allowing other plants to grow larger and healthier.

Orange daylily flowers present a striking sight along country roads in July.

The familiar, orange daylily makes a long-lasting floral display each summer along Maine's roads and in gardens.

Select only firm, young tubers. These can be dug any time of year, and if the stand were protected from freezing by a layer of straw, the opportunistic forager could conceivably go out in sub-freezing weather, shovel away the snow and dig fresh daylily tubers.

Finally, the young tips that protrude from the ground in early spring are edible when lightly steamed. I don't bother with them, though, preferring to wait until summer, when the flower buds offer such a fine reward.

Common daylilies offer an abundance of wonderful food products and their simple beauty makes it easy to have them near us.

Oxeye Daisy

When asked to draw a flower, most people will make a daisy because that's what comes to mind first. Oxeye daisies are composite flowers, having a yellow disc in the center and white petals, otherwise called "rays."

As with so many other useful wild plants, oxeye daisies, *Chrysanthemum leucanthemum*, are native to Europe and were brought over, probably quite by accident, by early settlers. From that seemingly insignificant beginning, oxeye daisies have spread far and wide and can be found almost everywhere, along

Tightly packed buds make the best nibbles.

roads, driveways, lawn edges and in fields and meadows. Daisies have become ubiquitous.

For most people, oxeye daisies, otherwise known as just plain "daisies," have no use other than being a pretty wildflower and the source of simple but effective wildflower bouquets. And those alone would be sufficient to endear daisies to us for all time. But daisies have another attribute, one which most people are unaware. They make very good eating.

During my wild plant walks, I'll pick a handful of unopened daisy buds and ask participants if they are brave enough to nibble on one. Then, after everyone who wishes has tried them, I'll ask people what daisy buds taste like to them. The answer, if you don't already know, may come as a surprise. Daisies taste just like carrots.

We've seen such taste comparisons before. Clintonia leaves taste just like cucumbers. Still, it is unusual for a wild plant to have a taste similar to a cultivated vegetable.

I place daisy buds in the "trail nibble" category. That is, daisy buds need no cooking. Just snap the unopened bud off the stem and enjoy. Those who like carrots will probably love daisy buds. Just be sure to select the most tightly packed buds. Half-opened buds are not as good as more compact ones.

Daisy buds also go well in salads, adding color and flavor. But that's not all. Daisy foliage, too, incorporates that same carroty taste and when chopped and added to salads or other foods, add a distinct carrot flavor.

So the next time you see a stand of oxeye daisies, take a moment to stop and enjoy their simple beauty. Then snip a few buds and give them a try. I hope you'll enjoy them as much as I do.

Pearley Everlasting

Pearley everlasting, *Anaphalis margaritacea,* loves dry, upland settings. It grows on unkept sections of lawns, pastures, along dirt roads, in reverting fields and in sunny, woodland clearings. A familiar plant, instantly recognizable on sight, most people are not aware that pearley everlasting has a practical use.

Native to the United States, pearley everlasting was once cultivated in European gardens as a bedding plant. In fact, a great number of native American plants found their way to Europe, brought there for their beauty and also for their culinary properties. Oddly enough, some of these plants, while no longer popular in the USA, are greatly appreciated in their new homes across the sea.

Here again, this common wildflower need offer us nothing more than its simple beauty in order to deserve our esteem. However, Nelson Coon, in his 1963 classic, *Using Plants For Healing,* lists a string of medicinal uses for pearley everlasting. I have not tried any of these and don't intend to, since the uses seem to me somewhat tedious and perhaps a bit fanciful. But it satisfies me to know that this common wildflower was once used to treat such a wide variety of ills.

Medicinal properties aside, I have a favorite use for pearley everlasting, one that requires nothing more than kneeling down and picking the bright-white flowers. These globe-shaped flowers have dry bracts (looks like a petal) and a light-yellow center.

When walking in the woods in summer and early fall, my mouth often becomes dry. Some years ago, I discovered that chewing on pearley everlasting flowers stimulates saliva flow. At first, the dryness of the flowers seems more likely to contribute to dry mouth than to relieve it. But when chewed, the flowers soon work their magic and dry mouth vanishes. Chewing on these really does slake thirst.

Besides this, the flowers have a pleasant (at least I think so) taste and are worth chewing just for that alone. I much prefer chewing on freshly-picked pearley everlasting flowers over commercially-produced chewing gum.

Oddly, it seems that every time my mouth becomes dry and I begin to wish that I had carried a canteen of water, I find pearley everlasting along my way. This happens so frequently that I have come to count upon finding these pretty little flowers to satisfy my needs.

Pearley everlasting grows to a height of about three feet. The leaves are long and slender and grow alternately on a downy stem.

Taking this one step further, anyone trying to quit the habit of using tobacco snuff can benefit from pearley everlasting. Chew the blossoms until softened and then use them as a tobacco substitute, placing them in the "snuff pocket" normally reserved for the toxic plant product.

Oh, I forgot to mention that someone once told me that the blossoms made

Pearley everlasting is a woodsmen's chewing gum.

an acceptable tobacco substitute. I tried mixing these with the dried leaves of common mullein, *Verbascum thapsus*, but while the ersatz "tobacco" tasted good enough, it burned much too hot for my taste. I don't recommend smoking pearley everlasting.

Tansy

Tansy or *Tanacetum vulgare* grows in much the same settings as pearley everlasting. It also grows on the seashore, down to the high-tide mark. Leaves resemble ferns, and each leaf division has coarse teeth. Leaves are highly aromatic and emit a strong, spicy scent when crushed. Even young leaves of early summer have this property. Flowers, which appear in late summer, are flat, yellow discs, developing into flattened clusters.

Tansy has a number of medicinal properties and was also used in cooking, where British cooks made tansy cakes, a seasonal delicacy. But science declares tansy hazardous to our health and modern medicine discourages any internal use.

So what good is a plant that we dare not use internally? Well, one of the old-time medicinal uses was as a vermifuge, or something that rids the body of parasites. So, then, tansy's toxic properties make it a relatively effective insect repellent.

I enjoy the heady scent of tansy and always crush some and put in my shirt or jacket pocket and also stick a sprig or two under my hatband. The fact that it helps to repel pesky insects is just an additional benefit.

Another good way to use tansy is as a strewing herb. This age-old practice involves spreading freshly-harvested tansy (or whatever herb is to be strewn) on the floor so that it releases its volatile principle when people walk on it. I don't use it inside, mostly because it makes a mess. However, outside use is something entirely different.

When friends visit my place for a picnic in my wooded back yard, I always try and strew tansy on the ground around my picnic table. The scent pleases my guests and me and, hopefully, it helps to thwart mosquitoes and other insect pests.

Of course it's difficult to prove a negative, so I can't really take an oath that tansy truly does work in this way. But I think it does, and that's good enough for me.

The rare individual may develop dermatitis from handling tansy. I have never seen that happen, though.

Aromatic fern-like tansy leaves are used to repel insects.

In late summer, I like to pick tansy flower clusters and place them in a vase, *sans* water. They quickly dry, making for a dried flower arrangement that lasts all winter.

Elderberry

"Showy ornamental. Trouble-free. Berries great for pies, jellies, wine. Hardy to zone 4." That string of accolades is typical of the way seed and plant companies pitch their cultivated elderberry plants. And sure, they aren't misrepresenting anything. In fact, most ads leave out one or two other positive attributes of this excellent summer-flowering favorite.

Common elderberry, *Sambucus canadensis*, differs little from the cultivated variety. "Tame" elderberries grow larger fruits, but everything else remains the same.

People who live in cities, towns and suburbs would do well to plant a pair (two plants are needed for proper pollination) of elderberry shrubs. But those who have access to the practically unlimited number of wild shrubs growing along field edges, rural roads and country lanes, have only to stop and harvest the free, wild bounty.

In spring, elderberry bushes seem out-of-sight and out-of-mind. The tender branchlets have yet to assume their full stature and for the most part, faster-growing grasses and other wildlings overshadow the plants. But in summer, after elderberry

The white blossoms of common elderberry precede the dark-purple, antioxidant-rich, berry clusters.

In late summer, clusters of black elderberries hang heavily on bushes.

shrubs have attained their full height and the thickly-packed, flattened, flower clusters appear, elderberries become the main roadside attraction.

The ripe flower clusters have several uses. First, the clusters are the main ingredient in heavenly-tasting fritters. Again, describing the taste is beyond my ability. But suffice it to say, guests at my place, eating elder fritters for the first time, never turn down an offer for another plate of golden-brown elderberry fritters. In fact, even cold fritters have a short life expectancy, since they are bound to get eaten before they can be stored in the refrigerator. I have not yet encountered anyone who did not pronounce these fritters excellent. See the recipe for the fritters in the last chapter.

I often re-heat my elder fritters in a toaster oven (a microwave tends to soften them) and they are just as good as fresh. They also respond well to re-heating in a frying pan, with just a little melted butter.

Finally, cold fritters make a sinfully, self-indulgent midnight snack.

In addition to their use in fritters, elder flowers are an ingredient in an old-time cold remedy. This simple mixture calls for one part dried elder flowers, one part dried mint leaves and one part dried yarrow, *Achillea millefolium* blossoms. Mix thoroughly and store in a closed container. Use one teaspoon per cup of boiling water to make a healing tea.

In late summer, after the berries come on, country people haunt back roads, buckets in hand, picking wild elderberries. Most make jelly out of these small, tart berries. Others make wine. I make an entirely different product.

First, for anyone who likes wild jellies, just pick as many elderberry clusters as needed and then follow the directions that usually accompany packages of commercial pectin. I won't go into winemaking, either, but I will tout the virtues of elderberry wine.

My friend Dan is a superb winemaker and his most stellar product is his elderberry wine. This powerful drink has no hint of cloudiness and tastes much like the finest port wine. Dan has, several times, won first place in winemaking contests with his elderberry wine. Any dedicated winemaker can make a similar product. The only difficulty here is waiting for the wine to become ready for drinking. It is that good.

I don't make wine and seldom use jelly. But I still harvest ripe elderberries for use in cooking. Eaten out-of-hand, elderberries are unpleasant, musty-tasting. But drying removes any trace of strong taste, leaving only a distinct "elder" flavor.

Dry on a sheet of nylon window screen or on the bottom of a large basket. Store in any container, it needn't be airtight. The dried berries must reconstitute before use. While placing in boiling water for a short time would achieve that goal, I have found an easier way.

When using dried elderberries in a batter, which is my main use, just make the batter and then stir in the berries. Then, allow the batter to sit. It takes between ten and fifteen minutes for the berries to swell. After this, proceed as usual, with whatever the recipe calls for. Note that while other berries tend to color the batter (blueberries and blackberries are notorious for this), elderberries do not.

It seems such a shame, when the man on the tractor with his side-cutter bar drives down the road and cuts grass, weeds and sometimes, elderberry bushes. Surely, he doesn't realize his error. In the end, though, the plant wins, since it is perennial and will rise again, to provide food and medicine for foragers for another year.

Blueberries

Maine blueberries represent an important sector of Maine's agricultural economy. From the vast barrens of Washington and Hancock Counties to the smaller fields and hills of Mid-Coast and Central Maine, everyone has at least a passing acquaintance with Maine blueberries.

But Maine has another kind of blueberry, common, widespread and certainly as sweet and delicious as their better-known, low-growing cousins. These are highbush blueberries, *Vaccinium corymbosum*, and they grow on shrubs up to ten feet tall. Look for highbush blueberries on acid soil, near wetlands, along lakes and ponds and even along power line right-of-ways. Take care if picking on a right-of-way, since companies frequently apply herbicides to shrubs and trees.

Highbush blueberries produce so much fruit that one shrub, or bush, can supply a family's needs for an entire year. And picking couldn't be easier. No bending required here, just stand and pick. My method involves holding a pail under a berry-laden branch and stripping the berries in bunches, allowing them to fall in the pail. You might even place a sheet or tarp under a bush and simply shake the branches. The ripe berries will fall on the tarp.

One of my favorite fishing sites, a small, mountain pond that holds lots of big white perch, has become my prime highbush blueberry-picking location. Here, blueberry shrubs line the shore. And since white perch bite well in midsummer, when the berries are ripe, I like to combine an outing and pursue both fish and berries at the same time.

Picking these berries requires nothing more than taking a break from fish-

Highbush blueberries make picking easy, no bending required.

ing and paddling to shore. Then, without stepping from my canoe, I bend the branches down and holding them over a five-gallon pail, strip the berries with my fingers. The only way this could get easier would be if the berries picked themselves and hopped into my pail.

July stands out as a prime highbush blueberry month in my section of Mid-coast Maine. Even so, different sites have earlier berries than others and to keep track of this, I have begun recording ripe blueberry dates in my copy of *Forager's Notebook,* published by Just Write Books in 2011. This has an endless calendar and lasts for years.

I see in my notes, then, that the first highbush blueberries of the 2012 season were on Sears Island on July 7. The little mountain pond mentioned earlier saw fully-ripe berries on August 15, 2011. I didn't hit the pond in 2012, which accounts for the lack of an entry for that year.

Blueberries lend themselves to eating fresh, which is my favorite way of having them. Sometimes, I'll not even bother with putting them in a pail, but rather just stand under the bush and eat my fill.

However, blueberries, highbush blueberries included, are noted in dozens of recipes, from pancakes to muffins and preserves to jams. Some people even make blueberry wine. My favorite use for blueberries is in pancake batter. A stack of pancakes filled with fresh-picked blueberries and covered with lots of real Maine maple syrup makes a stick-to-your ribs breakfast.

And while dessert was never my high on my list, on the rare occasion when I indulge myself, I'll have fresh blueberries on ice cream. Frozen berries work as well for that purpose.

To process blueberries for later use, just clean the berries, being careful not to get them wet. Spread the berries out on a table and remove all leaves, sticks and insects and then place the berries in a freezer bag, no further preparation needed. Place the bag in the freezer and the berries, being dry, will freeze separate from one another. This allows you to remove just the desired amount of berries from the bag and then place the balance back in the freezer for another time.

By the way, highbush blueberries sometimes appear to have a darker shade of blue from the ground-hugging variety. But they are as sweet or sweeter. Do give them a try. I'm sure you won't be disappointed.

Beaked Hazelnuts

Some wild products are so good that we human foragers must contend with other species for the same prize. Animals, insects and who-knows-what all seek the sweet reward found in the prickly, elongated husk of the beaked hazelnut.

I long ago realized that procrastination doesn't pay, not when beaked hazel-

Beaked hazelnuts grow in clusters. The husks are prickly, so wear gloves when harvesting. The nut itself looks the same as commercially-offered filberts.

nuts, *Corylus cornuta*, come ripe. One year, I waited too long before harvesting the nuts that hung so heavily on the bushes along my driveway. Every single nut had a tiny hole, the mark of an insect pest that had arrived just ahead of me.

In Mid-Coast Maine, beaked hazelnuts come on any time from late July and into August. Hazelnut bushes somewhat resemble alders in form and stature. They grow to ten feet or so in height. The somewhat oblong, pointed leaves are doubly serrate, meaning that small teeth grow on larger teeth. In late spring, the plants develop dangling catkins.

Lacking any knowledge of the physical appearance of the shrub itself, one look at the nut serves to make a faultless identification. These come on in groups of two or three, joined at the base. The nut itself is hidden inside a bristly, prickly, pointed husk. The common name, beaked hazelnut, is quite appropriate, since the husk does resemble a long, tapered beak.

Don't try picking these nuts barehanded. The sharp spines cause much irritation, so always wear gloves, preferably leather gloves. It doesn't take long to pick a half-gallon or so of beaked hazelnuts. After that, the real work begins.

These are perfectly fine as they come off the bush. I sometimes allow the husks to dry before removing the nut. Either way, use gloves and a jackknife to trim away the husks. A nutcracker or even a pair of pliers breaks the nut open, revealing the meat. The nuts closely resemble cultivated filberts and, in fact, surpass them in taste.

Beaked hazelnuts prove the worth of diligence and industry.

Arrowhead

As with cattail shoots, harvesting arrowhead, *Sagittaria latifolia,* tubers requires some work, often in wet, muddy conditions. The tubers, when cooked like potatoes, make the work worth it. Still, I consider this one of the more difficult of wild foods to procure.

The best way to go about this is to use a long-handled potato rake or similar tool. Find arrowhead growing in shallow water. With the rake, allow the bent tines to sink into the bottom mud and then pull back, slowly, in order to dislodge the tubers. Swish them around as best you can in order to rinse off clinging mud and clay. Some people advise foragers to wade, barefoot, and dislodge the tubers with their feet. I tried this, but it was no use. Far better, I think, to wear waders or hip boots and harvest arrowhead tubers with a long-handled tool.

Anyway, arrowhead rates as a high-value plant for foragers. Look for them growing on pond margins, in the soft mud of slow-moving streams and in water-filled swamps. Watch in late summer and early fall, as the leaves turn brown and wither. Then, harvest all you can. Digging arrowhead tubers does no harm to a colony.

Here again, the botanical name, *Sagittaria*, which means, archer, befits the plant. The common name, too, has worth. The leaves have a definite arrowhead shape, except that the gaffs, those two slender, appendages on either side, are exaggerated when compared to a real arrowhead. *Sagattaria* leaves are held just above the surface of the water. In some instances, the plant grows in the muck along the edges of ponds or streams, especially in places that held water in late spring but pretty much dry up during prolonged dry spells in summer.

Locate arrowhead tubers by the plant's uniquely shaped leaves.

Any potato recipe works for *sagittaria*, so don't limit yourself to just boiling. Experiment with various cooking methods. If you can locate a nearby source of these one-inch tubers, they just might become a regular favorite.

Purslane

Once purslane becomes established in a flower or vegetable garden, one of two things must occur. Either the aggressive "weed" drives the gardener to distraction, or it becomes a cherished addition to the summer table. In my case, the latter proved true.

Regarding common purslane's botanical name, *Portulaca oleracea,* I once experienced a remarkable epiphany. It happened this way. I bought a six-pack of portulaca, the annual flower that adds so much color to rock gardens and flowerbeds. That was in mid-spring. That summer, purslane showed up in the same area. The similarity between the two was striking.

Both have succulent stems, fleshy leaves and both are low growers, seldom reaching more that a few inches above ground. But then again, purslane is, indeed, a form of portulaca, as indicated by the scientific name.

A non-native, purslane is supposed to have originated in India. It now grows around the world. In some countries, including the United States, forms of purslane are cultivated as a prized vegetable.

Purslane can, if given its head, take over a garden. Pulling the plant by its roots keeps it at bay, but that never fully eradicates it. Still, it makes sense to leave a few plants for table use. To use, just snip the stem tips. They'll grow back in no time, providing more purslane.

Look for a sprawling, vining plant, with succulent stems with a trace of

The paddle-shaped leaves and stems of purslane excel in stir-fry recipes.

red. Tiny, yellow flowers grow at the stem tips. The leaves are paddle-shaped, widest at the ends. The top of the leaf is shiny, dark green. The bottom of the leaf is whitish, looking for all the world as if it was coated with a white, metal-flake finish. Hold the leaf upside-down in sunlight and turn it about. It will seem to sparkle.

When purslane first appears in my garden, I like to pick the entire tiny plant, minus roots, and use it in a salad, along with whatever other wild ingredients I can drum up. This use alone would be enough to recommend purslane to the fussiest eaters.

Do note that thorough rinsing is a must. Purslane has the ability to pick up the tiniest grit particles from the soil, even if the soil doesn't appear gritty. Rinse, rinse again and then rinse one more time.

As the plant grows, it becomes suitable for other uses. The larger stems and leaves make a fine potherb. Just cut into manageable sizes and boil. Also, since it is slightly mucilaginous, purslane stems and leaves serve to thicken gumbos and soups.

My favorite use is in a stir-fry, either in combination with other wild vegetables or alone. Chop the stems into half-inch sections and drop into hot oil in a wok. Cook on high heat, stirring constantly, until well wilted. I like to drizzle soy sauce on my stir-fried purslane and then serve it on a dish of rice. A simple meal is this, but nourishing, very tasty and of course, free.

Purslane contains Omega-3 oil, the kind found in salmon and other fatty fish. This is in addition to an abundance of vitamins A and C.

The seeds can be harvested, dried and ground into a meal. I don't do that, simply because it is so tedious. But for those who love baking and would like to experiment with something new, purslane flour comes highly recommended.

Purslane lends itself to blanching and freezing. Speaking of which, it's too bad that my place is so small and space in my freezer so limited. That necessitates that I take great care in the selection of whatever wild plants I wish to freeze for winter's use. In the end, I usually choose a different variety each year, alternating from one wild favorite to another. Maine just has too many great edible wild plants.

Serviceberry

Serviceberry comes into bloom in early spring, just before leaves on deciduous trees unfurl. The pure-white blossoms stand out against a still-brown background. Most casual observers take these blossoms as those of wild cherries. Cherry trees don't blossom for several more weeks, though.

An interesting plant, serviceberry is both a tree and a shrub, depending upon its height. The difference between the two depends upon the plant's height. *Forest Trees of Maine,* Maine Department of Conservation, 2006, considers anything under fifteen feet in height at maturity as a shrub. Over that point, it's a tree. In fact, other than in the above-mentioned booklet, there is no hard-and-fast distinction, at least not to my knowledge. Most serviceberries of my acquaintance grow as trees.

Identifying serviceberry, *Amelanchier laevis*, in early spring is easy, since no other trees bloom at that time. Before blossoms appear, I find it simple to identify serviceberry by its tight, grayish bark and contorted stems, or trunks. The leaves are oval and quite finely toothed. To me, they resemble apple tree leaves, with their leathery appearance.

The berries develop in July, beginning as hard, red, blueberry-shaped fruits and later becoming soft and dark blue, even approaching black. In their prime, nothing beats serviceberries for a sweet, invigorating, out-of-hand treat. A trail nibble superb, serviceberries are.

Interestingly, some trees (or shrubs) produce better berries than others. The degree of sweetness varies considerably. None are bad, but some are far tastier than others. For this reason, I have my favorite trees, places where I visit each July and pick the delicious fruit. One such place, Sears Island, illustrates something else about serviceberries.

While serviceberry occurs throughout the state, often among hardwoods and along field edges and in mixed-growth woodlands, it also grows along the sea-

People sometimes argue whether serviceberries are large shrubs or small trees. Some varieties grow to 30 feet, but most are only 10 or 15 feet tall. Mature specimens exhibit twisted, crooked trunks.

Serviceberries shown here turn blue when fully ripe.

shore. So a clamming/foraging expedition to Sears Island often ends with me resting just above the high-tide line, in the shade of a serviceberry tree, nibbling on the tender fruit. So decadent, so comforting and so worth repeating each year.

These would probably make an excellent jam, pie filling and also ought to enliven any muffin. But the freshly-picked variety more than satisfies my cravings. It's just another case of everything in its time, enjoying seasonal produce as it becomes available.

Galinsoga, "Quickweed"

At the same time that Maine's seaside plants come into a useful stage of their development, many of our garden "weeds" are at a point where they demand our attention. One of these, galinsoga, *Galinsoga ciliata*, grows fast, out-competing cultivated crops. This habit of rampant growth accounts for the common name of "quickweed." *Galinsoga* is an alien weed that reached the United States by way of Mexico. Maine was among the last on the list of galinsoga's conquests.

Any plant that takes over our vegetable gardens, no matter how good it is in its own right, cannot remain. With galinsoga though, total eradication is impossible. The plant self-seeds so efficiently that despite our most diligent efforts to remove it, young galinsoga continually pops up, often within a few days of the most ruthless weeding and cultivating.

Galinsoga, an aggressive garden "weed" is a superb cooked vegetable.

Given galinsoga's aggressive behavior, it is well that it makes such a fine potherb. I pick leaves, tender parts of the stem and whatever flowers are present. This goes into boiling water and remains there at least ten minutes before being fully cooked.

Galinsoga retains much of its bulk when cooked, making it difficult to drain. So I like to let it sit in a colander while the rest of my meal is being prepared. When fully drained and served with butter, salt, pepper and a dash of either cider or white (in recent years, I have come to relish white vinegar and often use it in place of cider vinegar) vinegar, galinsoga becomes a first-rate vegetable.

I have blanched and frozen galinsoga and find it an excellent frozen vegetable. A half-dozen packages suffice to keep me in touch with this garden weed throughout the winter.

Galinsoga seldom grows much more than one foot tall and, in fact, the provident gardener should never allow it to get anywhere near that high. I recommend harvesting the plant when it is between two and four inches tall.

Galinsoga has opposite, coarsely toothed leaves, widest at the base and finely pointed at the end. Stems are hairy and forked. The flowers, tiny and quite insignificant, have a yellow disc, with five white rays. Each ray, or petal, has three lobes.

Note that while widespread in Maine, not all gardens have galinsoga. To remain free of this tasty yet aggressive plant, carefully scrutinize any garden soil or compost before adding it to your galinsoga-free soil. Once galinsoga gains a foothold, remedial action becomes impossible.

Lady's Thumb

I delight in introducing people to lady's thumb since this plant's common name is so surprisingly fitting. Each leaf has at its mid-point what looks like a dark smudge, perhaps made by a thumb.

So here in Maine, we say that the smudge or blotch was made by a Lady's thumb. But the Highland Scots of days gone by had another explanation. They maintained that the spot was caused by a drop of blood, which splashed on one of the plants during the crucifixion and has continued on every plant, to this day.

Lady's thumb, *Polygonum persicaria*, belongs to a group of plants known as smartweeds. Smartweeds get their name from the peppery bite evident upon tasting the plant. This flavor ranges from mild to quite hot, depending upon the plant.

Lady's thumb, though, lacks that hot aspect, a good thing for those who relish it as a potherb. The word *Polygonum*, by the way, is a combination of *polys*, many, and *gonu*, joint. Lady's thumb has jointed stems. Each joint has a thin, fringed sheath. This sheath covers both the stem and also the base of the leaf. Flower spikes originate at this joint, too. The individual flowers are tiny and of a pinkish-red color. Note that Japanese knotweed, covered in the section on springtime plants, is a *Polygonum*.

The leaves, besides having the distinctive smudge, are long and slender and sharply pointed. The leaves lack teeth.

The brown splotch in the middle of the leaf gives lady's thumb its common name.

Lady's thumb grows in damp soil, in wet areas along roadsides, moist, riparian habitats and even in gardens, if they are located on low ground. In fact, my vegetable gardens sit in a low area and it takes them ever so long to dry in spring. In 2009, Maine saw near-continually cold weather and rain throughout the growing season. Along with many other gardeners, all my crops failed. In fact, I was unable to even pull weeds, since walking between my rows just stirred up the mud.

Were it not for wild edible plants, I would have lacked fresh vegetables altogether. Lady's thumb found my soupy ground to its liking, and although the crops that I planted all died, the lady's thumb prospered. I was able, by walking around the perimeter of my beds, to reach in and harvest enough lady's thumb for regular eating throughout the summer.

Even now, the winter following a summer of famine, my freezer bulges with bags of fiddleheads, knotweed, dandelions, goosetongue, wild berries and wild mushrooms. This anecdote points out that while cultivated crops can and do fail, wild crops are nearly 100 percent dependable. Those who acquaint themselves with Maine's nutritious and abundant wild plants need never go without food.

Returning to lady's thumb, I eat only the leaves, the stems being too coarse. Lady's thumb loses some bulk in cooking, so take note. Cooking time is less than that required for plants with thicker leaves. I like to cook lady's thumb in boiling water for only about five minutes. Drained and serve with salt, pepper, butter and vinegar, lady's thumb is an excellent green.

While I prefer my lady's thumb cooked, the young leaves, raw, are tasty in salads.

Skullcap

A member of the mint family, but without a mint aroma, Skullcap, *Scutellaria lateriflora*, grows in wet areas such as streamsides, pond edges and even roadside ditches. Leaves are opposite and medium-toothed. Flower stems grow from leaf axils. Small blue flowers grow on only one side of these racemes, or flowering stems. The flowers are long and tubular, lipped on the outside. Their resemblance to the protective metal cap worn by ancient knights accounts for the common name, skullcap. Several other skullcaps grow here in Maine and I find *S. epilobiifolia*, or common skullcap, grows in a wet meadow on my land. Both these species have similar medicinal properties.

Skullcap can grow to three feet, but usually only ranges between twelve and fourteen inches. Not too sturdy, skullcap often grows among grasses and rushes, where it finds support for its somewhat spindly stem.

As for looks, skullcap is unassuming to the naked eye. But when viewed under a lens, the flowers are strikingly beautiful. When photographed with a

Skullcap, a natural tranquilizer, has a square stem, indicative of the mint family. The flowers while tiny are beautiful.

macro lens and transferred to a digital image, the flowers make a beautiful photographic subject.

A mild tranquilizer is made by steeping skullcap leaves and flowers in boiling water, following the usual proportions for a herbal tea. This tea aids in relaxation. I find it soothing for frazzled nerves, a real relaxer. Also, I like its bitter taste. This and other bitter herbs help digestion and act as a tonic. For these reasons, I make it a point to pick skullcap each year, place it loosely in a basket and hang it to dry on a cut nail on the beam in my kitchen.

Skullcap contains an active ingredient called *scutellarin*. This accounts for its sedative properties. As with any other drug, synthetic or plant-based, always check with your physician for any possible drug interaction or other indications.

Peppergrass

Peppergrass, *Lepidium* species, is a general term for a fairly large family of plants that share a common peppery taste. Horseradish, that cultivated root used to make hot sauces, is a type of peppergrass. Peppergrass grows in untended garden sites, on roadsides and even on unkempt lawns. It does best in poor soil.

My land hosts *L. campestre*, or field peppergrass. I frequently pick the leaves and add them, chopped, to garden salads. They add a pleasant highlight, only slightly spicy.

This is one plant that I don't purposely seek, nor do I pick it in any large quantity. It usually grows singly, so harvesting any great amount is not possible, at least not on my property. I allow peppergrass to grow here and there in my

Peppergrass makes a spicy trail nibble and exciting salad addition.

garden beds so that when I want a zesty nibble or a spicy addition to a salad, it is ready at hand.

Like its relative horseradish, field peppergrass contains a healthy portion of vitamins A and C, not surprising for a member of the mustard family.

Field peppergrass has deeply-toothed leaves that grow alternately, up and down the stem. The somewhat fleshy leaves are sessile, clasping the stem at their base. The tiny white flowers have four petals, as do all the mustards. After the flowers fade, the plant develops flat, nearly circular, cleft seedpods.

Peppergrass is not a big-time player in the world of wild edible plants, but definitely a plant worth knowing.

Lamb's Quarters

Lamb's quarters or *Chenopodium album* are near the top of my list of all-time favorite wild edible plants. Growing profusely on cultivated ground, newly-graded roadsides, and even old manure piles, lamb's quarters are ubiquitous. In fact, I have even spied it growing from a crack in the sidewalk in downtown Greenville and also in the half-whiskey barrels used to plant flowers in front of a grocery store in the town of Brooks. The whiskey-barrel plants were thick and healthy looking, tempting me to pick them and put them in my shopping bag. But not knowing what substances passers-by may have dropped in or on them, I resisted the urge.

Lamb's quarters taste like the mildest, sweetest baby spinach, picked early in the morning at the peak of perfection. Any meal, even a basic one such as

broiled fish and simple salad, is trans-
formed to epicurean fare when accompanied by a dish of cooked lamb's
quarters.

Odd, isn't it, that such a common
plant elicits such eloquent praise? But
that sort of thing happens all the time
with our wild edible plants. Something we labor to grow and cultivate
with our sweat and time cannot compare in quality to the rank "weed" that
arrives unbidden and grows despite
our efforts to eradicate it.

And yes, lamb's quarters is the
kind of weed that takes over gardens.
It sets seed abundantly, firmly estab-
lishing itself for years to come.

Here's how I deal with lamb's
quarters in my garden beds. The plant
begins growing sometime in early May,
and near month's end is perhaps four or

*Nearly every garden plot has its resi-
dent lamb's quarter.*

five inches tall, just right for picking. It being so tender at this young stage, I
pull the entire plant up by the roots, shaking off any clinging dirt and dropping each little plant in my harvesting basket.

Later, back in my kitchen, I trim the roots off each plant, usually by lining
them up so the roots are even and doing a handful at a time. Then they are
placed in a colander and thoroughly rinsed. But, like jewelweed and orache,
lamb's quarters is "unwettable." Still, rinsing removes any dirt or other foreign
objects. Then, it takes but a few minutes of simmering in a slight amount of
water to cook these tender young greens.

This first annual helping of lamb's quarters has turned into something re-
sembling a quasi-religious function. "How long has it been?" I ask myself.
"A whole year. And now, here we are again, in late May, with the first lamb's
quarters meal of the season." I silently and reverently eat my meal, happy to be
alive and well in the great state of Maine in glorious springtime.

As much as I rave about the superb culinary aspects of lamb's quarters, a
19th century British writer once said"

> *The fleshy leaves were once boiled as greens, but they are probably
> little used now, as they form but an insipid dish, decidedly inferior to that
> made of the common nettle.*

I'll bet that this writer had never tasted lamb's quarters. In fact, it's for certain that he felt himself superior to those country types who had no choice but to harvest and eat the rough weeds that grew all around them. Such condescension has no place in a discussion of our wonderful edible, wild plants of Maine.

Lamb's quarters, along with other members of the group *Chenopodeae*, were commonly known as "goosefoot," owing to the shape of their deeply-toothed leaves. In Britain, lamb's quarters was specifically termed "white goosefoot." This alluded to the white mealy powder that covers the leaves. That same grainy-feeling substance is found on orache, which accounts for that plant's common name of "seaside lamb's quarters."

By midsummer, any lamb's quarters that managed to escape weeding have grown to several feet in height. I purposely leave a few plants for summer use. These I manage by picking only the most perfect leaves and tender tips. Such pruning tends to make the plant bushy and branched, encouraging even more tender growth.

These adult lamb's quarter plants provide another service in addition to their culinary use. The plant is a virtual magnet for leaf miners, those troublesome insects that disfigure green, leafy plants by eating their way through the leaf, leaving translucent, white, curlicue trails. Devoting one lamb's quarter plant to the miners allows cultivated plants to grow, relatively unscathed.

When cooking lamb's quarters, it is imperative to err on the side of caution. Less is more here. Again, since these dainty leaves cook so quickly, it makes sense to save them for last. When everything else is nearly ready, boil only about a half-inch of water in a saucepan and dump in the lamb's quarters. Stir to ensure even cooking and notice that the leaves immediately turn a lighter, more attractive shade of green and become very limp. The process takes no more than two or three minutes, tops.

Drain well and serve with butter, salt and pepper. This wild vegetable far outshines any of its domestic counterparts. It is so good, that were I allowed to freeze only one wild plant for winter's use, it would have to be lamb's quarters.

To freeze, blanch, but do so very quickly. Drain and drop blanched lamb's quarters in ice-cold water and stir, so it cools as rapidly as possible. Removing excess moisture, freeze as per my recommended, two-bag method. Immediately place in the freezer and then congratulate yourself on a job well done. Later, when blizzards howl, those frozen lamb's quarters will go far to rekindle the memory of sunny summer days.

By the way, if you have too many lamb's quarters in your garden and haven't time to weed them, my number is in the phone book.

Green Amaranth

An unwelcome invader from south of the U.S. border, green amaranth, *Amaranthus retroflexus*, is a real bully. An annual, amaranth sets out flower spikes that bristle with countless, prickly spines. It self-seeds rampantly. Its stem, while smooth, is stout, unlike other weeds that favor the cultivated ground in our vegetable and flower gardens and also farmer's fields.

But green amaranth has one virtue that appeals to me. Its leaves make a fine potherb. These leaves are dark green on top, with a reddish tint on bottom. They lack teeth and instead have slightly wavy edges, or margins. Green amaranth, if left to go to seed, grows up to two feet tall.

Who, having seen this stalwart, rough plant and felt the prickle from bristly seedstalks, would guess that it could make such a mild and agreeable vegetable? Young leaves, gathered throughout the summer and cooked for at least fifteen minutes, are a suitable potherb for even the daintiest palate.

As with so many other alien plants, if green amaranth doesn't grow on your land, it probably won't arrive there without human intervention. Again, commercial compost, topsoil and old, rotted manure are suitable mediums for green amaranth to grow in.

Indeed, the amaranth in my vegetable garden, as well as a few other edible weeds, are relative newcomers. Some years ago, a local farm began manufacturing and selling compost. This consists of a mix of cow manure and topsoil. The topsoil, of course, had seeds of every weed known to grow in the area. It was, in effect, an "instant weed garden." Lucky for me and others who imported this weedy product into their gardens that most of the hitchhiking weeds are edible.

The leaves of green amaranth, known globally as a grain product, make an excellent potherb.

Getting back to green amaranth, while it is unwise to purposely introduce any such aggressive, invasive plant to where it didn't previously grow, there is nothing wrong with foraging on existing sites. In much of Maine, green amaranth grows abundantly on commercial fields. Look for it especially on fallow ground. A harvester could easily pick a bushel of leaves from such places, in just a short time.

Most gardeners despise green amaranth and do everything in their power to rid their ground of it. But as long as it is already there, why not try eating it? You might find, as I have, that it is quite tasty, far better than some of the cultivated greens that we so dutifully tend.

Joe-Pye Weed

The sight of blooming Joe-Pye weed always elicits a tinge of sadness. Joe-Pye weed, *Eupatorium maculatum*, blooms in late summer and, for me, serves as a precursor to the coming fall.

Joe-Pye weed is a remarkable specimen plant and provides good service at the back of the perennial bed, a foil for shorter plants. The leaves, borne in whorls of four or five, are coarsely toothed, growing to ten inches or more and pointed. The stem is either entirely purple or has purple blotches. The flowers, pinkish-white, grow in large, flat clusters atop the plant. The entire plant grows well over six feet.

Even if Joe-Pye weed had no practical use, its beauty and stature certainly would make it something that everyone can appreciate. But it is also a fairly effective medicinal plant, one with a long string of uses. I employ a strong tea of the leaves to fight fevers, colds and the flu.

While no perfect cure exists for these common maladies, some wild medicines are at least helpful. I consider Joe-Pye weed among the useful medicinal plants.

As with all plant medicines, this one has a shelf life of no more than one year. This makes it necessary to go out each summer and pick and dry enough Joe-Pye weed leaves for a year's use. Rituals such as this add flavor to the changing seasons.

While I use only the leaves of Joe-Pye weed, the root is also widely

The pinkish-white flowers of Joe-Pye weed are the harbingers of autumn.

used medicinally. But since the leaves work just fine for my purposes, I'm content to forgo the spadework required to harvest the roots.

Joe-Pye weed grows in wetlands, along streams, shallow ponds and sometimes along the edges of swamps.

Jewelweed

Think back to the spring and those small jewelweed (*Impatiens capensis*) plants that we picked and used as a cooked vegetable. Now, in summer, those tiny plants have grown to four feet tall and sport bright-orange tubular flowers that depend, or dangle, from thin stalks. Also, seedpods, ripe and filled with seeds, have their own tender stalks. These long, cylindrical pods, tapered at the end, burst at the slight touch from curious human or passing animal. This habit of shooting the seeds gives the plant its common name of "wild touch-me-not."

While the smaller leaves are still edible, the time for eating jewelweed has long passed. Now, the plant serves as a poison-ivy antidote, an extremely effective one.

The succulent aspect of jewelweed, while evident in early spring, is quite obvious now. Just break one of the stems and feel and see that it is completely moist inside. The plant holds a remarkable amount of liquid.

The most basic way to use jewelweed against poison ivy (and other rash-causing plants) is to pick a few stems and crush them in the hands. Then, rub the resulting juice on any bare skin that might have had contact with poison ivy. This in-the-field remedy keeps the poison at bay, at least until the skin can be more thoroughly washed with soap and water back at home.

The effectiveness of this treatment has been shown to me time and time again. Here's an anecdote regarding the last time jewelweed's worth was so ably proven. My friend Tony stood on a bridge over a small stream, casting to fish below. He hooked a brook trout and not wanting to chance losing his prize by attempting to reel it directly up to the top of the bridge, Tony climbed down to the water's edge so that he could land his fish safely.

But in climbing up and down, he didn't notice that he had passed through a bunch of poison ivy growing on the bank. Tony said that he was extremely sensitive to poison ivy and would soon break out in a terrible rash. Looking around for jewelweed, which I found growing near the bridge, I told him not to worry. Tony applied the jewelweed and we continued fishing. Later, he reported that he did not develop the expected rash.

Needless to say, Tony is now a firm believer in the prophylactic properties of jewelweed. Such incidents occur all the time.

For those who have already developed a poison ivy or other similar rash, jewelweed can still help. Pick a large bunch of the plant, including stems, leaves, seeds

In early spring, it's easy to fill a basket with young (3-5 inches tall) jewelweed. Moisture beads up on leaves and sunlight makes these droplets shine like jewels, thus the common name.

and flowers. Break these up and place them in a large saucepan to simmer until the water turns dark brown and evaporates to the point that only about one half remains. Then, allow to cool and then drain the liquid into a bowl or jar. Wash all affected areas with this solution as often as possible. Keep the jewelweed liquid refrigerated. It will remain effective for about twenty-four hours. This also helps to shorten the duration of irritation from insect bites.

Sometimes the dry air of winter, especially in houses heated by wood, causes our skin to become dry and itchy. At this point, it's too late to go out and pick jewelweed to help us. But we can turn to the freezer for relief, if only we have a supply of jewelweed ice cubes.

Make the jewelweed tea as mentioned above and, when cool, pour into ice cube trays and freeze. Later, remove the jewelweed ice cubes from the tray and place them in a freezer bag. Freezing the liquid preserves and keeps the active ingredients fresh and effective almost indefinitely. To use, melt one or two ice cubes in a washcloth and dab on the itchy skin. Or, add two or three ice cubes to bath water and have a long, relaxing, jewelweed bath.

Hopefully, you will never have to resort to jewelweed as treatment for poison ivy and other rashes. But if and when the need arises, jewelweed is always there, ready to serve.

Wild Parsnip

One year, I neglected to pull all the parsnips from a bed at the edge of my lawn. These lived over winter, to grow again the following spring. Again, I forgot about them and by the time I took notice, they were fully mature and had developed large, flat seed heads.

Digging these made no sense, since parsnips become woody once they set seed. So I left my now-wild parsnips to go another year. But being biennial, they later died. The seed that they dropped, however, germinated and gave me some perfectly fine parsnips for later on.

In time, I moved the soil from this bed to a sunnier location and completely forgot about my unintentional parsnip experiment. That is, until I began seeing something like my wild parsnips growing in fields, along the edges of people's lawns and even on parking lot edges. Were these parsnips? I had to find out.

Later, while visiting a friend, I noticed a number of these parsnip-like plants in a field bordering his lawn. They looked like regular, cultivated parsnips, with the long, grooved stalk and divided, toothed leaves and flat, yellow flower clusters on top of the stalk. Digging the plant revealed the truth. Here were plain, old parsnips, legions of them, spread around for hundreds of feet.

So why bother to plant parsnips when they grow so abundantly in the wild? Well, cultivated parsnips have one thing over the wild variety, that being the

Wild parsnips are simply domestic parsnips gone wild.

condition of the soil. When we sow a root crop, we do so in well-tilled, deep, loose soil. This encourages quick growth and also a shapely, well-formed root. Wild parsnips grow where the seed falls and often this can be on hard ground in waste areas. This often leads to stunted or otherwise unusable roots.

Even so, where you find wild parsnips, you usually find a lot of them. And at least some of the wild variety will have decent, well-shaped roots.

Note that some people may develop a long-lasting rash from exposure to parsnip leaves. It's best to wear long sleeves when working with parsnips.

By the way, the botanical name is *Pastinaca sativa*.

Soapwort

Soapwort, *Saponaria officinalis*, is inedible and it has no medicinal properties. But this is a book about useful plants and soapwort is, indeed, useful. That use may be inferred from the common as well as the botanical name, which means to saponify, or produce soap.

Besides this, soapwort is a hardy perennial, able to stand up to the harshest Maine winter. It produces rose-scented, pinkish-white flowers, most often double. The leaves lack teeth and grow opposite on a stout stem.

I often locate stands of soapwort while walking along from one trout stream to another, or while foraging for edible plants, solely by their sweet aroma. When that happens, it makes me smile. I'll always stop and sniff the flowers, too.

A native of Europe, *Saponaria* was once a common garden plant. I grow a stand of it in a small, narrow flowerbed in front of my house, where it delights my senses from July through late summer. But in general, soapwort has faded

A few soapwort leaves agitated in a jar of water makes an alternative to soap.

The entire plant, when crushed, added to water and shaken, produces a mild soap. It was used historically as a shampoo.

in popularity and few people bother growing it today. Its once universal acceptance, though, is evident by the huge stands that grow along roadsides, along railroad tracks, powerlines and around old homesteads and cellar holes. These plants have, all of them, naturalized, escapees from long-ago gardens.

Anyone interested in historical gardens is well-advised to consider adding *Saponaria* to their inventory of plants. Its use dates back to Europe and one of its common names, Bouncing Bet, comes from the name used for barmaids in old England. In America, people grew it for both its beauty and also to use as soap.

This is not just any old soap, either. It is gentle enough for the most delicate fabrics. In fact, it is used to restore ancient tapestries and other historical fabrics.

To make an instant soap, just grab a handful of leaves, stripping them off the plant. Crush them, tearing with the fingers and place them in a glass jar. Fill the jar halfway with water, screw on the cap and shake vigorously. Soap bubbles appear as the process of saponification begins its work. Use this soapy water in emergencies and also just for the delightful experience of making and utilizing your own soap from a wild plant.

Soapwort grows best in semi-shade. My plants, however, stand up to full sun quite well.

By the way, the reason for naming this plant after British barmaids? It is thought that they washed their drinking vessels in a soapy solution made of *Saponaria*.

Staghorn Sumac

If it weren't a common wild shrub, staghorn sumac, *Rhus typhina*, would probably be propagated and sold as a landscape shrub or small tree. The compound leaves, with their opposite blades, add a tropical look and the ripe seedheads, with their hairy-looking berries, contrast nicely with the dark-green foliage. The long fruit clusters, borne on the end of branches, persist through the winter, adding style and color to an otherwise stark, white landscape.

Once, during a plant walk, a participant asked me if I had ever eaten staghorn sumac branches. Well, I hadn't but was willing to try. Then that person began separating young, supple branches from where they attach to the trunk, peeling the fuzzy (thus the "staghorn" in velvet stage common name), bark. This left small, white, tender shoot-like sections that tasted like nothing else in my experience. It was delicious.

Harvesting this small shoot only works in spring because after that the branches become too tough. Also, sumac branches contain a white, sticky sap, similar to that found in common milkweed.

The real heavy hitter of staghorn sumac are the berries. These spire-shaped clusters are filled with tightly packed, fuzzy berries, and it is the berries that make such an exceptional and refreshing beverage.

Staghorn sumac berries when soaked in cold water make ersatz lemonade.

People liken sumac-aide to pink lemonade, but it's a good bet that anyone drinking this for the first time and with their eyes closed, wouldn't make the pink-lemonade analogy. The stuff tastes exactly like lemon juice, pink or otherwise.

To make this ersatz lemonade, snap off several berry clusters and carefully examine them for clinging debris and also, any insects that may have found the berries to their liking. Then gently roll the clusters between your hands, slightly crushing the berries. After this, place the berry clusters in a pitcher, cover with cold water and let steep for about 15 minutes. The water will acquire a light red cast at that point.

Then strain the reddish-colored liquid through a fine strainer or even a section of cheesecloth. That removes any remaining debris. After that, cool in a refrigerator and serve as lemonade, sweetening to taste with honey or maple syrup.

Despite the pink-lemonade aspect of this fine drink, it also has a much more utilitarian use. That is, it can supplant lemon juice in any recipe calling for lemon juice. It even works well on salmon, trout and other seafood.

One final note. Don't harvest the berries immediately after a hard or prolonged rain, since rain washes the acid from the berries and it is the acid that gives us that lemon flavor.

After trying staghorn sumac, I bet you'll develop a new appreciation for this handsome source of lemon-tasting liquid.

St. Johnswort

"It's yellow time." That's what I think when bright-yellow, St. Johnswort begins showing along the dirt road where I live. In late summer, a great number of yellow wildflowers brighten roadsides and St. Johnswort is prominent among them.

St. Johnswort, *Hypericum perforatum*, is a shrubby, European plant that has done an admirable job of naturalizing in Maine and much of the rest of the New World. It stands up to three feet tall, has small, paddle-shaped leaves. These leaves have little black dots, oil glands, visible to the naked eye, but far more impressive when viewed through a hand-held lens. These dots account for the second half of the botanical name, *perforatum*, or having the appearance of being perforated.

The flowers, too, have an interesting structure, due to their bristly group of stamens. These almost appear prickly, but really they are not.

Anyone who listens to radio and television has to have heard at least one advertisement for some St. Johnswort product. It's a big business, picking, putting up and peddling this wild perennial plant. One of the main reasons to buy this and other commercially-produced plant medicines is because they are of a standard strength.

Ancient herbalists used St. Johnswort as a remedy for depression.

St. Johnswort has a long pedigree of medicinal uses, probably the most widely-known being as an antidote for depression. I personally don't get so depressed that I need an antidepressant. But if I did, I would certainly turn to St. Johnswort.

My neighbor uses a tea made of both St. Johnswort flowers and leaves. He takes this regularly, throughout the low-light days of winter. He says that it helps him stay cheery. I'm sure it does, too.

Look for St. Johnswort growing on gravelly roadsides, fields and lawn edges.

As for now, I'm content to enjoy late summer drives along country roads and the bright-yellow blaze of that hardy herb, St. Johnswort.

Maine's Seashore

Maine's shoreline hosts a multitude of useful wild plants. In fact, they are among my very favorites, ones that I devote precious freezer space to in order to enjoy in winter. Some of these plants grow just above the high-tide line, kissed by salt spray, but rarely immersed. Others inhabit the intertidal zone and are not available unless the tide has gone at least partway out.

Some of these plants are best taken home and cooked. Others offer sumptuous trail nibbles. My coastal meanderings frequently take me past these "instant snacks." In fact, such impromptu lunches have become a much-anticipated part of my seaside walks.

Indeed, if people new to foraging only availed themselves of one single habitat, the seashore would offer the widest selection of edible wild plants. It is no stretch of the imagination to say that, at least in summer, Mainers have no reason to ever go hungry, as long as they have access to undeveloped stretches of seashore.

An introduction to wild edible plants of Maine's seashore wouldn't be complete without mention of the problems connected to people walking their dogs on the beach. This practice may please pets and their owners, but it pretty much puts the place off-limits for foragers. The thought of eating a plant that a dog has relieved itself on is discomfiting.

The only solution is to get off the beaten path, where casual strollers and their canine companions rarely venture. Avoiding popular public beaches helps, too. Finding wild edible plants on rocky or otherwise difficult terrain pretty much guarantees that the plants haven't been compromised.

Beach Pea

I know of no other wild plant that has a more specific window of opportunity than beach peas. Hitting this garden pea look-alike at just the right time usually requires two or more trips to the beach. But Maine's seashore abounds in wild edible plants, so no beach pea prospecting trip is ever in vain.

I usually find beach peas ready in my part of Maine by late June. Some places have earlier peas, some have later. Microclimates have much to do with this, whether or not the beach peas grow in a protected area, or stand out in the open, on a north-facing beach.

Beach peas bear a striking resemblance to cultivated peas and are used in the same manner.

Beach pea, *Lathyrus japonicus* grows on gravelly areas, as well as sand spits and strands, just above the high-tide line. The vining stem holds alternate (but sometimes opposite), ovate, compound leaves. The plant's similarity to garden pea or edible-pod pea vines is evident. If that weren't enough, beach peas develop pods, filled with tiny peas. These, too, look for all the world like something just picked from someone's vegetable garden, except the peas inside are much smaller than garden peas.

Discussing beach peas reminds me of the time I lived in a rented house and couldn't have a garden. Even if a garden were possible, not much would have grown because the place faced chilly, windswept Penobscot Bay. Back then, shorefront property was not worth a whole lot, it being cold and mostly with poor soil unsuitable for gardening. How times have changed.

Anyway, even though my diet was deficient in cultivated vegetables, it was filled with wild treats. And beach peas were certainly welcomed that summer. You would have thought that I had found a one hundred-dollar bill, I was that pleased to find a stand of beach peas at the perfect stage of ripeness.

Finding beach peas never poses a problem. Finding them ready for eating, as mentioned earlier, often requires multiple field trips. Harvesting the ripe pods is simplicity itself, loads of fun. The real work comes in shelling beach peas.

Select only peas that when removed from the shell are dark green and shiny. Removing these from the pod is best done with a swipe of a fingertip. This doesn't sound too difficult, but since these peas are so small, it takes many, many swipes to free enough beach peas for a meal.

Cook as per garden peas, in a slight amount of salted boiling water. It takes between eight and ten minutes for the peas to become tender. Overcooking doesn't do much harm, so err on the side of cooking too long rather than not long enough.

Beach peas are another one of those wild foods that should not be cooked until other components of the meal are nearly done. That's because beach peas lose their sweet taste when cold, so are best served and eaten while still piping hot. Use butter, salt and pepper and be ready to see your cooked beach peas perform a quick vanishing act. All the more reason to go out and pick another mess, while they are still ripe.

Sea Blite

Sea blite, *Suaeda maritima,* grows just above the high-tide line and, in fact, sometimes slightly below. Neither the scientific name nor the common names tell us much about this plant, except that it is a seashore, or maritime, species. We do know, however, that in addition to growing naturally in Maine, sea blite also occurs in Britain.

At first glance, sea blite looks as though it would feel prickly to the touch. The short leaves more closely resemble something seen on a spruce tree, rather than a tender and succulent edible plant. In this case at least, looks are deceiving. Locate some sea blite and feel its softness. The needle-like leaves as well as stem tips are very supple.

Sea blite develops tiny, green flowers in the leaf axils, the junction where leaves join the stem. These flowers are insignificant and don't add to or detract from the plant's overall edibility.

Look for sprawling, vining sea blite along both rocky and sandy shores and also saltmarshes. Not much else resembles this common seaside plant, so locating and identifying it should be fairly easy.

My favorite use, which by now anyone might easily guess, is as a trail nibble. The tender tips are laced with sea salt, which imparts a pronounced salty flavor. Persons who dislike salty food would probably want to rinse in fresh water before eating. Either way, just grasp the supple end of a stem and break it off with your fingers. It's easy to pick a large amount in only a short time.

Sea blite, a sprawling trail nibble, also serves as a cooked vegetable.

Sea blite, chopped and sprinkled on a salad, adds a certain zip and I highly recommend trying it that way.

Finally, sea blite makes a fine potherb. Just boil for at least five minutes, drain and serve with butter, salt and pepper. I like just a dash of either cider or white vinegar.

These are only a sampling of the various preparation methods that work for sea blite. I suggest that if you find this plant to your liking, you treat it the same as spinach and use it in any way you would spinach, which would include in soufflés, quiche and perhaps even an ersatz, oyster Rockefeller.

By the way, if you take sea blite home and don't have time to deal with it, it keeps well in the crisper drawer of a refrigerator.

Glasswort

A trail nibble of the highest magnitude, glasswort, *Salicornia,* various species, grows at and below the high-tide line. Frequently, entire stands are completely inundated during high water. The plant likes a hardpan-type soil, especially the clay soils so frequently found on the Maine seashore and along tidal rivers and streams.

Here is an instance of the scientific name providing solid information on the plant. *Sal,* means salt, which in this case, refers to salt inherent in the plant. And *cornu,* means horn, a reference to the prominent smooth branches.

Glasswort, (center) a crisp trail nibble, adds zest to salads.

Glasswort, like so many other seaside edible plants, has several uses. Again, the plant is best eaten raw. Slightly crunchy, with a clean, zesty salt flavor, it makes a superb trail nibble. I frequently visit a certain low area on the end of a faraway point, specifically to sit down and munch on glasswort. High water fills the low area where the glasswort grows, so my trips must coincide with low tide.

Upon arriving at my destination, I immediately head to one of the many tidal channels. There, in the middle, are hundreds of little glasswort plants. By mid-to late-June, the glasswort has grown to a usable size, perhaps two inches or so. It is good at any stage of development, but picking it when smaller than this involves way too much effort.

Oddly, over-indulging in this salty feast has yet to make me thirsty. Perhaps the difference lies in the type of salt, or perhaps it has something do to with the way it is absorbed into the system.

Minerals and trace elements must abound in a plant that spends time, twice daily, underwater. I'm convinced that incorporating glasswort into our diets would significantly add to the amount of beneficial vitamins and minerals that we all need. It would also, no doubt, preclude the need to take commercially-produced supplements.

I've encountered the rare individual who doesn't care for fiddleheads and have met many who won't eat dandelions. But never, ever, has anyone whom I introduced to glasswort had anything but praise for this abundant, uniquely-shaped, little plant.

Look for translucent, rounded, jointed stems that branch out from a main stem, opposite each other. The plant is succulent and generally erect, especially in early summer. It can, at later stages of development, develop a sprawling aspect. In summer the plant is a light shade of green, but in autumn it acquires a deep reddish tint, the seaside version of colorful autumn leaves.

As mentioned before, glasswort occurs in large colonies, so if you find one, you will have found many dozens.

Glasswort lends itself well to salads, too. Chopped and added to any salad, it imparts a wonderfully-complex extra dimension. Standing alone, chopped and splashed with salad dressing, glasswort is superb.

Finally, glasswort makes an outstanding garnish, particularly for seafood dishes. Chop up a handful of stems and sprinkle over broiled salmon or trout or mackerel. In essence, it complements any and all foods, a valuable plant indeed. And, just think, it's wild and free.

Before leaving glasswort, remember to break off the stem instead of pulling it up by the roots.

Sea Rocket

Writing this section in winter, with snow falling outside, makes me pine for summer and all those wonderful days spent on the Maine seashore, picking and eating wild edible plants. I find it possible, at least in part, to recall tastes. This may not rate as such a good thing, since such memories make me miss my seaside plants even more. One of my favorites, and one that I only wish I had a bagful of right now, is sea rocket.

My "secret" glasswort site, mentioned earlier, offers another bonus. A ridge of sand, pitched high up on shore by tides and sculpted by wind, is home to sea rocket. After loading up on glasswort, I always make it a point to nibble on a few of the succulent, fleshy, irregularly-toothed leaves of sea rocket. These have no apparent stem, but instead seem to grow out of the main stem. Sea rocket has smooth, rocket-shaped seedpods. These later dry and become brittle, allowing the seedpod to crack open and shed its hoard of tiny seeds.

Sea rocket grows singly rather than in colonies. However, places such as the above-mentioned sand ridge often hold numerous sea rocket plants. Rarely, does anyone encounter just one, lone sea rocket plant.

Sea rocket, *Cakile edentula*, belongs in the mustard family. It has small, purple, four-petaled flowers on the stem ends. And if the cross-shaped flowers weren't enough of a hint that here, is some kind of mustard, then one bite of the raw leaf, seedpod or tender stem would resolve the matter. The pronounced mustard flavor has a slight bite, not strong or unpleasant in any way, but certainly noteworthy.

Sea rocket comes on sometime in June and by late August has nearly gone past its prime. I consider this plant valuable enough to not only stuff myself with it while sitting on the sand, I also take a good amount home for further use.

Sea Rocket has a tangy, mustard flavor.

I like to chop the leaves and use them as a garnish for roast beef or ham. A sandwich of thin-sliced beef with chopped sea rocket and perhaps a very thin slice of red onion and a dash of mayonnaise make a lunch worth remembering.

Salads benefit from a few handfuls of seedpods sprinkled in among the other ingredients. While this works well with traditional garden salads, by now it should be evident that enough edible plants grow along the seashore to make a totally wild salad. Consider tossing together chopped sea rocket, glasswort and a slight amount of sea blite. This heady combination could serve as a main dish or a robust seaside salad.

I don't cook sea rocket, since I can't get past using it raw and in salads. Others have, of course, prepared sea rocket by boiling in a slight amount of water.

Orache

What do spinach, beets and Swiss chard have in common? They are all related to the wild seaside orache. To my way of thinking, orache is somewhat sweeter and certainly milder than any of its domestic relatives.

Orache, *Atriplex patula*, is one of several members of a group of similar plants occurring on both sides of the Atlantic. The British knew *A. Patula* as "spreading halberd-leaved orache." That description fits the plant well, since orache leaves are shaped like a halberd, or wide spearhead,

The tender leaves of orache make a sweet cooked vegetable.

To further explain that image, look on the bottom of the leaf and find, on either side, a large projection, actually what we would otherwise call "teeth." These resemble the barb on an arrowhead or spearhead. Also, the leaves, especially on the bottom side, are covered with a bluish-white substance that has a mealy feel when rubbed. This substance allows the leaves to become completely immersed without getting wet.

Orache sometimes grows over two feet tall, with a sturdy stem and many smaller branches. But it also occurs, especially in more shady locations, as a spindly plant that can barely support itself. These variations make it important to identify the plant by the leaves, as described above.

Orache grows profusely, just above the high-tide line. Often, orache manages to grow through and even push aside dried rockweed and other debris thrown up on shore by extra-high tides and storms.

Vegetable gardeners, particularly those interested in non-hybrid plants, are familiar with red orache, a cultivated variety. When I first learned of this plant, the thought of having fresh orache in my own garden thrilled me. No more driving to the seashore for wild orache. The end result was very disappointing, though. My cultivated red orache didn't compare favorably with the wild type. It simply didn't taste as good. But this concept holds true in so many instances. Wild strawberries are infinitely sweeter than cultivated varieties, as are wild blueberries and so on. In most instances, wild is better.

While orache never thrilled me as a trail nibble, it certainly excels in salads. Perhaps we can list it as a fourth ingredient in our seaside salad described in the section on sea rocket.

As good as orache is in salads, it is a superb potherb. When steamed or cooked in a slight amount of simmering water, drained and served with butter, salt and pepper, it is a vegetable without peer. In an effort to explain just how good cooked orache tastes, I consider domestic spinach a very poor substitute for wild orache. If given a choice between the two, orache would win every time, without question.

Orache is one of those essential wild plants, something that I like well enough to pick loads of in summer and freeze for winter use. It keeps well, without any noticeable loss of flavor. There is something to consider, though, before going out to pick orache for freezing.

Orache cooks down, or loses some of its bulk when cooked. I can't offer a specific formula for this process, because there are just too many variables. In order to get a real feel for this, it pays to cook a given quantity of orache and see how much it shrinks. This knowledge pays off both when blanching the plant for the freezer and also when cooking for immediate use.

To pick orache, select entire, young plants. Just pinch off near the base. As the plant grows, pick the leaves and tender tips. I sometimes use my fingers as a rake, pulling along the stem and in the end, gaining a handful of leaves. The flowers are tiny and grow in leaf axils. They are edible as well, but I prefer to harvest only the leaves and tender tips.

Anyone who enjoys sweet, mild greens should pick as much orache as possible, at least the first time out. Then go home, rinse the plant and cook a quantity, keeping watch on how much bulk the plant loses in cooking.

Finally, don't stuff orache in a bag or other container. This makes the leaves sweat and makes it difficult to prepare later. Instead, use a large basket or canvas bag and make sure your orache is loosely packed.

It's tempting for me to list orache as my favorite wild edible plant. But so many others vie for that distinction that it's an impossible decision. I'll list orache up there in the "top ten" though.

Goosetongue

Goosetongue, *Plantago juncoides*, also called seaside plantain, occurs naturally in Maine and also Europe. I have found little to indicate that Europeans ate seaside plantain, but they did save the seeds and fed them to caged birds. This they also did with seeds of common dooryard plantain, *P. major*. The two plants have nearly identical seedstalks. The leaves differ considerably, though.

Goosetongue, or seaside plantain, has long, fleshy, slender leaves that come to a sharp point. These leaves are neither round nor flat, but cupped. A cross-section would resemble the letter U. Leaves typically average about four inches long, although they frequently reach six inches or more. Identify the plant, then, by both

Goosetongue, related to common plantain, grows at or below the high tide line.

the leaves and also, the seedstalks. But in early summer, before seedstalks appear, the leaves provide the sole means of identification.

In fact, early summer, mid-June in the Mid-Coast region, offers the best picking. Later, the forager must discriminate between leaves and seedstalks. Better to separate the two at the shore, rather than back at home. Now, though, it's easy to just break off (or cut with knife or scissors) the leaves at their base. The plant, being perennial, grows back and, in time, it would be hard to discern that a forager had taken a quantity of goosetongue leaves.

And it is the leaves, the dark green, succulent leaves, that we here in Maine are so fond of. Old-timers referred to goosetongue as "shore greens," a fitting, if quite general, description. Goosetongue grows singly and also in vast groups.

Look for goosetongue around the high-tide mark and also below it. The plant grows on hard-packed soils as well as rocky, gravelly areas. As with sea blite, a daily immersion in seawater imparts a salty tang to the plant. Goosetongue grows almost anywhere, as long as it can find tidal water. A tidal river only a few miles from my home satisfies all my goosetongue needs, and they are considerable. I love the stuff and not only eat it fresh throughout the season, but also freeze large quantities for winter use.

In fact, freezing does not appear to alter either the taste or structure of goosetongue. My freezing method of using two separate bags, explained earlier, works remarkably well for goosetongue.

As mentioned above, old-timers were well aware of the table qualities of goosetongue. But many of the old-time coastal residents have departed to do their foraging on a new shore and their descendents appear to have no knowledge of the free, delicious wild plant that their ancestors so highly esteemed. A tragic thing really, considering the bountiful vitamins and minerals available in a helping of goosetongue leaves.

Hopefully, a new generation of Mainers, people attuned to the benefits of our state's wild edible plants, will once again take advantage of our abundant supplies of this plant.

My seaside walks most always include taking time to pick a few helpings of goosetongue. The leaves compact well in the basket or bag, but this does not hurt them. In fact, my favorite basket, when filled with goosetongue leaves, has a noticeable heft. Because these succulent leaves are so dense, they do not shrink much in volume when cooked.

To prepare, I first clean goosetongue leaves by holding under cold, running water. This removes any clinging chaff or foreign matter. Next, it pays to chop the leaves into inch-long sections. This can be done later, at table, and isn't absolutely necessary at this time.

Bring a saucepan of water to a rolling boil and add whole or chopped goosetongue leaves. Cook for at least ten minutes, drain and serve with butter, salt, pepper and a dash of apple cider vinegar. The vinegar isn't essential, either, but I like it.

Unused cooked portions are easily re-heated in a microwave and taste nearly as good as fresh cooked, so don't worry about making too much at one time.

While I sometimes nibble on raw goosetongue leaves, they are not my favor-

Mature northern bay bushes make attractive specimen plants. They can grow twelve feet in height and circumference.

ite trail nibble. However, they do go well in a salad. Try adding some chopped, goosetongue leaves to our by now well-populated seaside salad.

Goosetongue definitely ranks up there in my top ten list of favorite plants.

Northern Bay

A Mason jar in my kitchen cupboard holds a winter supply of dried leaves of northern bay, *Myrica pensylvanica*. These I use in all recipes calling for Turkish bay leaves. This includes soups, stews and as a flavoring ingredient in steamed blue mussels. I add a few leaves to the water when cooking lobster, crabs or shrimp and also pack northern bay leaves in the jars along with fish slices when making pickled fish and also pickled eggs.

Leaves of northern bay don't taste exactly like Turkish bay leaves, of course. I personally consider our wild northern bay far superior to the store-bought product and consequently no longer buy or use Turkish bay leaves.

While picking some wild plants can be tedious, picking northern bay requires only that the harvester reach out and pluck leaves from the shrub or bush, no kneeling, bending or stretching required.

The species name, *Myrica*, traces back to myrio, meaning to flow. This may possibly refer to the shrub (sometimes northern bay grows tall enough to qualify as a tree) being found near water. In Maine, northern bay usually occurs within one mile of the sea and often very near the water. For this

The shiny leaves of Northern bay rival imported Turkish bay in flavor.

The waxy, gray "berries" are really nutlets. They can be rendered for candle wax and also, dried as a seasoning for meats.

reason I list northern bay as a plant of the seashore.

The leaves are nearly round at the end and widest near the middle. They lack true teeth and instead have some rudimentary notches. These exhibit some reflective properties and thus are difficult to photograph in bright sunlight. The leaves are very thin, and when examined with a hand-held lens, may exhibit resin dots.

Branches are woody, stiff, even at the ends. The fruit, really nutlets rather than true berries, are covered with a bluish-white, waxy substance. This, when rendered by boiling the nutlets in water, is used in candle-making and accounts for that unique "bayberry" scent associated with candles from coastal New England. The wax was and to some extent is, also used in soapmaking.

While the leaves are highly aromatic even when young, they are the most potent when fully developed. I like to wait until July before harvesting my leaves. In fact, my annual pilgrimage to the center of a certain island has become a traditional rite of summer.

A forty-five-minute hike takes me to a reverting hayfield, ringed on its edges by northern bay and sprinkled here and there with sweetfern. These venerable bay shrubs are as wide as they are tall. Some of them reach well over ten feet in height. By judicious pruning of the very tips of the branches, I am able to help these magnificent plants retain their symmetry while at the same time supplying myself with a year's worth of fragrant leaves.

Then, satisfied that I have harvested an ample supply, I stick a sprig from a branch tip in my shirt pocket in order to revel in the heady aroma during the hike back to my car.

Back home, I hang the branch tips on a beam in my kitchen, in a shady spot where air circulates freely. It takes less than one week (unless a humid airmass arrives in the meantime) for the leaves to become totally dry and brittle. At this point, I remove them from the branch tip to which they are still attached and drop them, one-by-one, in a glass jar. I take pains not to break the leaves, since they are liable to shatter and become unusable.

The bay-leaf jar then goes into my cupboard, on a shelf where other herbs are stored.

Dealing with bayberries is a busy project, one that I have not yet found time for. Perhaps someday, though, I will render some wax and hand-dip some northern bay candles. However, I do gather the nutlets, or "berries" along with the leaves, since they contain the same aromatic properties. These go well in cooking when used in the same manner as the leaves, adding them to soups and stews and when steaming or boiling blue mussels. Begin with perhaps five or six berries at first, so the bay flavor does not overpower the dish. After this, adjust berry amount according to taste.

Fall's arrival irritates many of us. If only it would hold off for another month or so. After all, summer is so very short. But by the time fall officially hits, most of us in Maine have already experienced a killing frost or two.

By now, most wild edible plants have come and gone, having completed their life cycle by growing, reproducing and dying. Tender plants have succumbed to the kiss of frost, but some hardier types persist. For me, early fall represents my last opportunity to gather medicinal plants.

So along with cutting and stacking firewood and going on those last few fishing trips of the season, I cast about for wild medicinal plants. And while fall brings glorious, sun-splashed days under cerulean skies, nights are cold. A few sticks of poplar or white birch in the woodstove serve to take the chill off. But there is little time. A sense of urgency prevails.

Goldthread

Goldthread is one of those plants that everyone who spends time in the Maine outdoors has seen, but few can name. A perennial groundcover, the shiny, green, tri-parted leaves closely resemble those of wild strawberry. But the resemblance ends there. Goldthread, *Coptis groenlandica*, produces no sweet fruit. It does, though, offer us a powerful medicine with which to thwart minor illnesses.

These brilliant-yellow roots grow just under the surface, in a vast latticework. They are, of course, thicker than the thread alluded to in the common name, but not by much. Limp, with little rootlets the length of them, these roots are easily pulled from the loose, forest loam by hand.

Picking goldthread roots is fairly easy, no tools required. Just find a stand of goldthread and scratch the leaf litter to where you get a handhold. Pull up a plug of this loose soil and look closely. It contains countless yellow roots. Break up the clump and slowly separate the roots by pulling with a steady pressure so as not to break them. Look in the shallow hole left by the divot you just removed and see more roots sticking out from the sides. Work these loose and add them to your container. Keep at it until you have at least enough to fit in two cupped hands.

Next, back home, spread the roots out on a table, separate them and remove any obvious bits of dirt or chaff. Now, pull each root through your fingers in order to remove those tiny, hairlike root fibers. After a thorough cleaning, rinse the roots and place loosely on a wooden cutting board to dry.

To digress for a moment, these roots are sometimes referred to as "canker root," owing to their ability to relieve pain of canker sores and other irritations of the mouth. For that purpose, just pull the roots from the soil, brush off any clinging duff and chew. Immediately, you will experience the clean, bitter taste and your canker sore will stop hurting. Chewing goldthread root also works for relieving minor sore throat pain. The stuff truly acts like a wonder drug.

But it is fall and no one knows when snow will arrive, dashing any hopes to gather more goldthread roots. So we must preserve what we have picked.

Now, given that the roots you rinsed have dried, take a sharp knife and cut them up as finely as possible. A tedious task, but worthwhile, given the value of the finished product.

After chopping the roots, place them in a glass jar. The size of the container makes little difference, since that all depends upon how many goldthread roots you have prepared. After stuffing the cleaned roots in the jar, cover them with vodka. Stir the roots in order to remove any trapped air, cap the bottle and place it in a dark cupboard or closet. Let stand for at least two weeks, the longer the better. I let mine steep for a month.

Next, look at the vodka and see that it has assumed a lovely shade of yellow. Drain the liquid into another container and discard the spent roots. I like to use two different types of containers to store my goldthread extract (that's what you just made by steeping in alcohol…an extract). First, I like to have a medicine dropper bottle full. These are available new in medical supply stores, but I re-use old ones that came with homeopathic medicine and they work perfectly fine. Some homeopaths might feel that the "resonance" of whatever first came in the bottle still remains. I don't think it does and, if so, it is of such infinitesimally quantity that it is of no effect.

Bright-yellow roots of goldthread grow right beneath the forest loam.

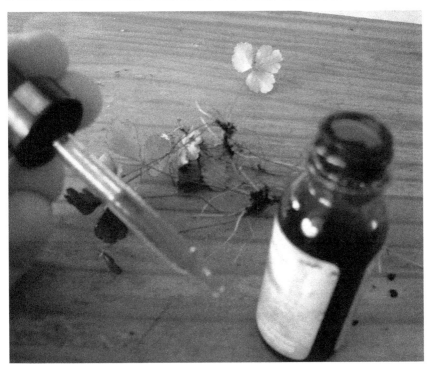

Goldthread tincture helps ease sore throats and cold symptoms for the author.

When I have a scratchy throat, I just fill the dropper and, with head back and mouth open, squeeze two or three drops in my mouth. It quickly trickles down over the hurting area, soothing as it goes.

For more firmly-established sore throats, I like to have a spray bottle filled with goldthread extract. For this, I buy a pump-bottle of cold and flu medicine, dump the medicine down the sink and wash the bottle with hot water. After all traces of the yucky, cold medicine are gone, I fill the bottle with goldthread extract.

A few good pumps provide temporary relief for scratchy throats and even stubborn sore throats. Of course, this is not an immediate cure, only a method of relief for the symptoms. Goldthread does have antibacterial and anti-inflammatory properties, though, so it very likely does contribute to the general healing process.

The stuff that makes the roots yellow and serves as the medicine in goldthread is called berberine. It occurs in several other wild plants, including yellowroot, *Xanthorhiza simplicissima*. Yellowroot was over-dug in its native range (it never occurred in Maine as far as I can tell, but in states farther south) by wildcrafters trying to eke out a living from nature. Now, people cultivate yellowroot and sell it at high prices. I find that free, plentiful goldthread serves my needs as well as expensive, commercially-obtained yellowroot.

Boneset

Surely an odd-looking plant, boneset, with its twinned leaves that appear as if they are fused together and the stem going through the middle. That perception accounts for the scientific name, *Eupatorium perfoliatum*. The first half of this tongue twister refers to an ancient Greek king, Mithridates Eupator, who supposedly used boneset medicinally. The second part, *perfoliatum*, indicates the perforated appearance of the leaves.

Wetlands, moist ground and in fact, most riparian, or streamside, habitat serves to support boneset. It grows thickly, all around my farm pond. The plant grows fairly tall, about two feet around my place. The leaves, which occur opposite, stick out horizontally on the stem. This horizontal feature imparts a three-dimensional, stately aspect to the scene.

In early fall, when I harvest my boneset, the plant bears small, white, fluffy flowers, arranged in flattened clusters. When fully opened, these clusters add to the plant's visual appeal. I prefer to pick boneset just before the clusters open, since that's when I consider it at maximum strength.

Boneset, a close relative of Joe-Pye weed, is used the same way and has much the same ability to cure a host of ills. I use it in a tea to bring on a sweat in order to help break a fever. Stronger, or excessive doses are extremely laxative, which explains another of the plants common names, "thoroughwort."

Learn to recognize boneset by its twinned leaves.

As with Joe-Pye weed, I harvest the leaves and dry them in a basket in my kitchen. When dried, I place them in a sealed container in my herb cupboard.

Often, years pass by without me needing any kind of fever medicine. Still, I go out each year and pick my boneset for "just in case."

Canada Goldenrod

Goldenrods of all sorts abound in Maine and New England. These belong to the same family as daisies, that being *Compositae*. But there, for many goldenrods, the similarity ends. The physical structure varies greatly, from graceful, bushy plumes to many-branched and even spire-shaped.

Fortunately, one of the more common and useful goldenrods has some hallmarks that make it fairly simple to identify. Canada goldenrod, *Solidago canadensis*, has features that make it an easy find. Look for a wavy plume of bright-yellow flowers atop a four-foot stalk. The alternate leaves have a prominent midrib, edged by less defined ribs, one on either side. The leaves are long, narrow and sharply toothed.

Herbalists attribute a number of medicinal properties to Canada goldenrod. They are probably correct, too, but I avail myself of only one use. The flowers, when chewed fresh, bring relief to a scratchy, sore throat. I also harvest and dry the flowers for use in tea during the off-season.

Goldenrod is unjustly blamed for hayfever symptoms, but ragweed blooming at the same time, is the real culprit.

The goldenrods bloom in late summer and continue through mid-fall. Unfortunately, common ragweed, *Ambrosia artemisifolia,* also comes into bloom at that time. Ragweed pollen triggers allergic reactions in many people. But ragweed is inconspicuous, while the goldenrods are extremely conspicuous. So, naturally, goldenrod gets blamed for most of the misery caused by common ragweed.

Honeybees, however, recognize goldenrod as a prime source of pollen. Since goldenrod is one of the last wildflowers standing in fall, bees work feverishly, gathering pollen to make honey. It is their last hurrah, so to speak, for the season. Goldenrod honey ranks as one of the best varieties.

Peter Henderson's comment on goldenrods, in his book *Henderson's Handbook of Plants And General Horticulture,* was visionary "The beauty of the plant would warrant its cultivation, had not nature's hand rendered it entirely unnecessary."

Henderson had no way of knowing that in the late 20th century, florists in Europe would recognize the worth of goldenrods in floral arrangements. The practice soon spread to the United States.

Bright yellow wands of Canada goldenrod graced my kitchen table long before I began noticing goldenrod in commercially-produced arrangements. The tall, graceful goldenrod works well along with other, seasonal wildflowers, particularly New England aster, *Aster novae-angliae.*

To me, the natural beauty of our wildflowers far excels the showy flash of hybrid cultivated types. A vase or even a water glass filled with such as what grows in Maine's roadsides, woods and fields gives me pause to stop and count my blessings. And, of course, one of our great blessings are the useful wild plants that give us food, medicine and just plain enjoyment.

Wintergreen

When the scientific name of a plant resembles a person's surname, chances are that it was, indeed, named for a person. In the case of wintergreen, the scientific name honors a Dr. Jean François Gaulthier, a Canadian. Wintergreen, *Gaultheria procumbens,* numbers among our hardiest of plants.

Even in winter, if push came to shove, I could walk outside my house and with a shovel dig down to where I know wintergreen grows. And there I'd find it, just as fresh as the day it was first covered with snow late last fall.

Wintergreen forms a dense mat of shiny oval leaves that have a leathery feel. These grow in bunches at stem tips. The leaves are normally a dark green, but in spring many of them turn a deep red. Interestingly, I have observed that the leaves that have turned red are those that got covered up by leaves from hardwood trees the previous fall, or else leaves that just grew beneath other wintergreen leaves. Those leaves that were not covered did not turn red.

Chew wintergreen leaves for a burst of flavor.

Wintergreen leaves run about one inch long, perhaps slightly more. They have fine rudimentary teeth, but these are not obvious.

Wintergreen flowers, small, white and bell-shaped, dangle, or hang down, below the leaf clusters. Later, the plant produces bright-red berries. Both the leaves and the berries are edible.

I like to chew on wintergreen leaves (I'm convinced that the red leaves have a stronger flavor than the green ones) while walking through the woods. While it wouldn't hurt to swallow the spent leaves, it is better to spit them out after squeezing the wintergreen flavor from them. Despite prolonged chewing, the leaves remain tough and leathery. But the flavor realized from just chewing them makes them a natural alternative to chewing gum.

Sometimes, a cup of wintergreen tea helps to brighten my day. It takes a lot of leaves to make a good, hearty tea. For one cup of tea, fill the cup half full of leaves and let steep in boiling water. Use the same proportion of leaves to water when making a pot of wintergreen tea. Allow plenty of time for the hot water to draw the wintergreen flavor from the leaves.

Wintergreen berries, which come on in fall, persist unharmed over winter and make a fine snack or trail nibble at any time, from fall to early spring. They have a grainy texture, rather pleasant, to my way of thinking. The wintergreen flavor is quite pronounced in the berries and only two or three are sufficient to impart a wintry blast of wintergreen to the inquisitive forager.

Wintergreen, along with other native woodland plants, has finally gained recognition by the general public, but not necessarily for their culinary aspects. Groundcovers, low-growing plants that provide a large area of visual appeal to a patch of shady ground, have become a desirable addition to many properties. To that end, rather than harvest from the wild, many companies now cultivate our native groundcovers for sale to landscapers and homeowners.

One catalogue advertises wintergreen as having bright red fruits, white, bell-shaped flowers and lustrous, dark-green leaves. Of course everything stated here is true and then some. It seems that for some who do not have wintergreen growing on their property, buying a few plants from a commercial grower makes lots of sense. This particular company has a price of $7.95 on one plant. Since wintergreen spreads by underground runners, it probably wouldn't take long to become established.

Find wintergreen in the shaded woodland, so don't look for it out in the open.

The next time you are walking in the woods and see a stand of wintergreen, why not stop and sample the leaves and berries? It's a pleasant experience, just one of many available from the useful wild plants of Maine.

White Pine

Maine, the Pine Tree State. In fact, an image of the white, or "mast" pine, is depicted on our state seal. While various species of pine occur in Maine, the state motto refers specifically to white pine, *Pinus strobus*. Pine played a key role in the settlement of our state, providing boards for building houses and barns and also timber for masts of sailing ships. In Colonial days, the tallest, straightest white pines were blazed with a mark depicting a broad arrow, denoting that from then on, England's Royal Navy destined it for their particular use. Of course this heavy-handed policy caused much consternation among independent-minded Mainers, since Britain made no distinction between pine trees on Crown lands and those on privately-owned property.

Sawmills large and small consumed vast amounts of white pine and, even today, pine continues to play a major role in our forest economy. In addition to its numerous uses as a building material, white pine bestows yet another boon to anyone willing to partake. The needles are the source of a pleasant, vitamin-laden tea.

Rather than take vitamin pills to increase my vitamin A and C intake, I much prefer to sip on pine-needle tea. Just select the tenderest needles, take them home, chop them fine and use in a tea. The amount of needles to tea varies according to personal tastes, but I find two heaping teaspoons of fresh-chopped

Chop and steep white pine needles for a soothing and vitamin-rich tea.

Chopping white pine needles exposes the plant material to boiling water making a stronger and more flavorful tea.

needles to one cup boiling water much to my taste.

My house sits in a little valley, surrounded by ancient white pine. In summer, gentle breezes make the needles "whisper." Also, my pines, especially those on the north ridge, afford much protection from the desiccating winds of winter. And at any time, driving in to my place, the visitor is immediately treated to the sight of a mature stand of Maine's number one wild plant—white pine.

So you can easily see why pine-needle tea means so much to me. You, too, can enjoy this simple pleasure any time of year. That's the gift of the white pine to us.

Eastern Hemlock

Eastern hemlock, *Tsuga Canadensis*, a stately, 60-70 foot tall tree, is widespread but scattered throughout Maine. The lumber, heavy when green and very strong, has many uses, including being used for framing and timbers for building.

But as foragers, we only deal with the leaves or needles. Hemlock, like white pine, was once favored as a readily available tea and was a favorite of old-time woodsmen.

To identify Eastern hemlock, look for small, slightly oblong cones suspended by short stalks. Leaves, from 1/3 to 2/3-inches long, are flat, with a very short petiole, or stem, dark green on top and whitish on the bottom. The arrangement of the leaves on the twig makes it appear that the entire twig is flat.

The bark is deeply fissured and resembles that of several other trees, so it is best to stick to the leaves and cones as identification points.

In some areas, mostly along the coast, a foreign, invasive pest does extensive damage to hemlock trees. The insect is wooly hemlock adelgid. It gets its name from the white, wooly coating that surrounds twigs and the insects themselves. However, wooly hemlock adelgid has not yet become a full-blown problem. But if you encounter a hemlock with these cottony-looking masses, call the nearest Maine Forest Service office and report your finding.

Gathering hemlock leaves is easy. Just twist the twig end and snap it off from the tree. Remove the needles by hand rubbing. These needles are what we use for tea. If possible, select young, light-green leaves for the best taste.

As with white pine needle tea, just add a scant handful to a cup and pour in boiling water. The amount of plant matter varies according to taste, and the only way to achieve the best results is by experimentation. I like my hemlock tea quite strong, but that's my personal preference.

By the way, don't confuse our native, eastern hemlock with the hemlock that poisoned Socrates since they are two different species. The potion that killed Socrates originated from a perennial plant, and that plant bears no relation to our hemlock trees.

Identify hemlock by its flat leaves or needles.

Hikers, people on the Appalachian Trail, for instance, have easy access to hemlock leaves. This beverage not only supplies a hot, tasty treat, but it also brings with it a heaping portion of Vitamin C. When harvesting, just take the tender, young tips, something that does not harm the tree at all. By making a cup of hemlock tea while on the trail, people are re-living a page from Maine's early days when people made regular use of such wild delicacies as hemlock leaf tea.

By the way, when locating a hemlock tree in winter, make sure to look on the ground for a thick layer of severed twigs. These cut twigs are the work of porcupines. A porcupine will set up residence high up in an eastern hemlock tree and spend perhaps months gnawing and eating. But even this does little more than trim, or prune the tree.

So please give hemlock tea a try. You'll instantly create a connection to the old days, and besides that, it tastes just plain good.

Beechnuts

If beechnuts grew as large as walnuts, there would be few or none left for grouse, squirrels, black bears and other nut-eating animals, because humans would gather them in vast quantities before the animals could get to them.

But, sadly, beechnuts are only ½-inch long and come enclosed in a prickly burr. The upside of this is that each burr usually contains two of the triangular-shaped nuts.

Beechnuts, *Fagus grandifolia*, the fruit of the American beech tree, have something in common with mushrooms. That is, their abundance appears cyclical. Some years the woods are full of beechnuts and other years, there are none.

But during those times when beechnuts come on in huge numbers, it takes only a short time to gather a sufficient quantity from the forest floor. And that brings up an important point. Beechnuts are best eaten after they fall from the tree. This precludes the need to climb trees and pull nuts from the branchlets.

Of course bears appear not to know this and so make it a habit to climb beech trees and feed upon the not-quite-ripe nuts. Often, trees where bears have foraged exhibit claw marks as a result of the bruin's visit.

As with many other wild delicacies, the capricious nature of beechnuts only adds to their allure. Are they worth the wait? Are they worth the admittedly tedious effort required to pry the nuts from the burrs and open them? Well, just ask anyone who has ever sat down and worked on a basket of beechnuts and that person will answer, "Absolutely."

Healthy beech trees have a smooth, gray bark. Others, and that incorporates the great majority of trees, have rough, canker marks on the otherwise pristine bark, a sign of beech bark disease. This, while it stifles tree growth by shortening

When not infected with beech canker, the bark on beech trees is smooth and gray, with some white flecking. The triangular nuts are enclosed in a prickly burr, usually two nuts per burr.

Beechnuts have prickly burrs.

their lives, in no way impairs the quality of the nut. Beech leaves grow alternately, average about four inches long and are coarsely toothed.

I consider beechnuts an ephemeral delicacy, best enjoyed while in season and not meant for hoarding or putting by for later use. Thus, by having no concrete expectations regarding whether or not they will appear on any given year, you can reap the maximum pleasure from each, sugary-sweet nut when you do find them.

An anecdote regarding a long-ago quest for beechnuts seems fitting here. One very dry fall afternoon, a friend and I set out looking for beechnuts. This was on one small corner of a huge, intact forest. But we didn't worry about getting lost, since we had only to turn around at a stream that flowed about one half mile from the road.

We went in different directions so as to cover the most ground. My friend turned around and headed back to the road and our waiting car at the appointed time. I kept going, looking for the stream. But soon darkness overtook me, with no sign of a stream. Clearly, I was "turned around" and so began making preparations for a long, chilly night in the woods. But while placing fir boughs in a little depression that would be my bed for the night, I heard the sound of a distant truck going down the road.

Listening as intently as possible, another vehicle went down the same road. Using the last vestige of dwindling twilight to view a distant tree as a guide and listening for another truck, I headed out of the woods.

It was somewhere around nine o'clock at night that I broke out of the brush and onto the road. As luck would have it, there was my friend. He and his wife had been cruising up and down the road, hoping against hope to find me.

We verbally sparred for many years later regarding whether or not I was truly lost or just turned around.

My friend has long since passed away, but that night and our search for beechnuts that we never found, remain among my most vivid memories.

Wild Mushrooms

Summer brings more than just leafy plants to Maine. Fungi abound and some years, forgers reap a bounteous harvest. Woods, lawns and roadsides all yield their corps of edible, wild mushrooms. It's a time of plenty and, on good years, nature provides us with so much that we can scarcely handle the load.

Since some wild mushroom are toxic, even lethal, it is imperative that we learn the identity of each mushroom to an absolute certainty. Simply holding a freshly-picked mushroom next to a photo and comparing the two is not enough. Every specific detail must match, even minute ones. Only then can we be one hundred percent certain of the identity of a new mushroom.

At that, it is unwise to eat a large portion of any new wild mushroom, even when we know that it is perfectly safe. Different mushrooms act differently upon different people. Some perfectly fine mushrooms cause problems if consumed with alcohol, for instance. So the best way to try a new mushroom is to take only a small portion, say a teaspoon or so, and cook it in oil, margarine or butter and eat it. Then, if no upsets develop, try eating a larger helping. Wait at least a full day, though, before doing this.

Does all this sound scary? It's supposed to. Yet, that should not stop anyone from pursuing this interesting and productive hobby. Many of our finest wild mushrooms are easy to identify and are difficult to confuse with any toxic species.

The way to become acquainted with our wild mushrooms is to learn them one at a time. Become totally and perfectly familiar with a single mushroom. Learn where it grows, what type of habitat it requires. Make notes as to when it is ready, since these dates remain roughly the same year after year. In time, these mushrooms can become regulars on our forging lists, eagerly looked-for and highly appreciated.

For those seeking a wider knowledge of Maine's wild mushrooms, I recommend a trip to the bookstore for a good field guide to wild mushrooms. I like the *National Audubon Society Pocket Guide to Familiar Mushrooms*, not only for the photos but also for the tables of spore prints. That is but one of a host of excellent field guides. Just make sure that whatever you buy includes spore print lists.

Mushrooms multiply by dropping tiny spores. These vary according to color. Knowing everything else about a mushroom except the spore print is of no help in making a totally accurate identification. But when all other criteria match, such as type of gills, shape, color, texture and so on and then the spore prints match up to the tables in a field guide, identification is complete.

To make a spore print, remove the cap from any cap-style mushroom and place it gill-side down on a piece of white paper. Place a waterglass over the cap and then leave it alone. It may take a whole day, according to the species, to drop spores. Later, examine the spore print and see if the color matches what your field guide says for that type of mushroom.

Some mushrooms, being of a different shape, do not lend themselves to making spore prints.

The six different mushrooms present in this book are among the most common and easily identified of all. None of them are the typical cap-and-stem type mushroom, but, instead, have strikingly different shapes. These are very easy to recognize. I recommend beginning with them.

Shaggy Mane Mushroom

My introduction to shaggy mane mushrooms was entirely by accident. While doing selective cutting on a seaside property, I noticed some unusual mushrooms growing on a grassy area. And although I had never seen this type of mushroom before, I immediately recognized the mushrooms as shaggy manes and went to my truck to find a container. The well-prepared forager always carries something to hold unexpected finds and so I placed my shaggy manes in a cardboard box.

Shaggy mane mushrooms decompose quickly as can be seen in the photo above.

Shaggy mane mushroom group.

How did I know these new mushrooms were shaggy manes? Because pictures of them from different mushroom guides came to mind. There is nothing else that looks like a shaggy mane mushroom. Of all the edible mushrooms, except those in the puffball family, shaggy manes are the easiest of to identify.

Shaggy mane mushrooms, *Coprinus comatus*, are somewhat ovate, looking like a stretched-out hen's egg. The strikingly different cap is covered with something like scales or short feathers. This feather-like texture gives the impression of an old-time lawyer's wig. Another analogy would be with a Scottish feather bonnet, the kind worn by Scottish military bands. The only difference is that feather bonnets are black and shaggy mane mushrooms are white.

Shaggy manes are cap-type mushrooms, but the stalk is hard to see until the mushroom is picked. The cap, rather than being solid, is hollow, which leaves a space between the stalk and the inside of the cap. A workable analogy compares the cap to a skirt or a dress.

Shaggy mane mushrooms grow singly but in often-large groups. Sometimes it is possible to harvest many dozens of mushrooms from a single colony. But don't plan on saving shaggy manes for use later, because they don't keep well. After a few days in the refrigerator the mushrooms become soft and if left alone, will turn to a black, inky mass.

So eat shaggy manes as soon as possible after picking. And if you are fortunate enough to find shaggy manes growing on your lawn, don't pick them until you are ready to prepare them.

Look for shaggy mane mushrooms on gravel parking areas and lawns. I once picked shaggy manes on a gravel bank overlooking Penobscot Bay.

Shaggy manes make their presence known sometime in late August or early September. They often persist through fall and well into November.

To prepare shaggy manes, check thoroughly for any specks of debris. Since these mushrooms grow upright, they should already be pretty much debris-free. If there is any gravel or grit on the bottom of the stalk, remove it with a toothpick, the point of a jackknife or an old toothbrush. But don't wash them, since that will soften the mushrooms.

I fry shaggy manes in the butter substitute "Olivio," but cooking oil works fine, as does real butter. Cook on low-to-medium heat, stirring often. While cooking, shaggy manes produce a dark liquid. This liquid, along with the cooked mushrooms, goes well over toast or a bed of rice.

Shaggy manes are capricious in that they may or may not show up in the same place year after year. Also, they are likely to pop up in new places. Essentially, any day you find a group of shaggy mane mushrooms is a very good day.

After cooking, shaggy manes can be frozen. But with such an ephemeral treat, I think it best to eat them fresh and appreciate them for what they are, a will-o'-the-wisp, that when located, gives some of the best eating around.

Chanterelles

Here in Maine, chanterelle mushrooms, *Cantharellus cibarius*, provide fresh eating from midsummer through mid-fall. These egg-yellow to gold mushrooms grow to a maximum of four inches in diameter and about two inches high.

The cap is generally flattened, but usually becomes depressed in the center, even to the point of being funnel-shaped. Blunt, wide-set gills adorn the outside of the cap and continue at least halfway down the stem. Some writers say that chanterelles exhibit a marked scent of apricots. That has never been apparent to me. Perhaps my sense of smell is just not acute enough to detect the apricot scent.

Common in hardwoods and also mixed-growth woodlands so typical of much of Maine, these mushrooms grow singly, meaning that while you may find many of them growing close together in a small area, they do not appear in clusters. They grow on the ground and because of their bright color, are easy to spot, even from a great distance.

Never pick any orange mushroom growing in clusters from the base of a tree, since that is how the toxic Jack-o-lanterns, *Omphalotus olearius*, grow. Beside that, Jack-o-lanterns have very fine, or thin, closely-set, or "crowded" gills.

Once chanterelles appear, they represent a crop that just keeps coming. Flushes of chanterelles closely follow summer rains and consequently, dry seasons often see few, if any, chanterelles.

But when conditions permit, these delicious mushrooms grow in great profusion, providing many meals over a long season. For that reason, chanterelles are one of my staple foods, reliable and predictable.

Given that chanterelles thrive in relatively wet weather, it should hardly come as a surprise that garden slugs, so prolific and so abundant during wet, Maine summers, find chanterelles to their liking. Which means that it pays to make frequent, regular visits to the chanterelle woods so as to harvest chanterelles before slugs can destroy them.

Of course slugs do not poison the mushrooms, but instead do material harm. Any remaining mushroom is safe for eating. But who wants to set tooth to something that a slug has partially eaten? Certainly not me. Oh, I have cut away nibbled areas from otherwise large, healthy chanterelles. But that is the extent of it for me.

Harvesting is easy. Just grab the stem at ground level and pick. With any cap-style mushroom, it pays to harvest the thing intact so as to make a positive identification. A large clump at the very base of the stem signals a poison mushroom.

Chanterelles are familiar summertime mushrooms that grow in mixed-growth woodlands. Easy to recognize by their external gills and yellow, waxy-feeling caps. Chanterelles grow on the ground, singly. Avoid any orange mushroom that grows in clumps.

Being thick and meaty, it doesn't take many chanterelles to satisfy a normal appetite. For me, three or four good-sized mushrooms suffice to make an excellent side dish. These I cut up with a paring knife and sauté in butter until tender.

In addition to either main course or side dish, chanterelles make an excellent addition to scrambled eggs. Many summer mornings see me making a breakfast of fresh chanterelles and eggs, capped off with cups of hot, black coffee.

Cleaning chanterelles involves some care. The gills, though wideset, harbor little bits of dirt, moss and other forest litter. But washing these woodland treats will make them soft and unpalatable, so clean them in the dry state. I often use nothing any more sophisticated than the tip of my pocketknife. A small brush, even a toothbrush, works well for flecking bits of dirt and duff from between the gills.

After cleaning, I find that chanterelles keep well in the refrigerator for three or four days, so it isn't absolutely necessary to eat them on the day of picking. Often, especially in times of scarcity, it pays to harvest whatever is available and go out two days later and collect more to add to the pot.

While chanterelles number among the tastiest mushrooms and the easiest to locate and identify, I find that just the sight of these brilliantly-colored mushrooms is ample reward for a morning spent tramping the Maine woods. And that's saying a lot for any wild mushroom.

Black Trumpets

"Look out, Tommy, those are death trumpets." That stern warning from my grandma clinched my long aversion to these sinister-sounding, but totally safe and delicious fungi.

With a name like, "death trumpets," who could blame old-timers for being afraid of them? But again, this only demonstrates the often-misleading nature of common names. And as much as to contradict that statement, another of this fine mushroom's common names is, "horn of plenty."

It all goes to underscore the importance of learning mushrooms one-by-one, inside and out. In the case of death trumpets, horn of plenty and the other common name, "black trumpets," this mushroom is truly one well worth getting to know.

The scientific name of this common mushroom, *Craterellus fallax*, serves as the best description of all. The first half of the two-parted name suggests a crater and indeed, the cap, as it were, is funnel-shaped, a true "crater." And the rest? Well, a bit of research will point out that "cornucopia" is the proper name for "horn of plenty."

This mushroom, though it grows on the ground in profuse quantities, has the maddening habit of blending in with dead leaves, sticks and forest litter in general. Thus, this writer has more often than not, walked by, past and even upon, many pounds of *Craterellus fallax* and not even known it.

Happily, once discovered, black trumpet locations often continue to produce for many years. So once found, a "trumpet spot" deserves revisiting each summer. And summer, late July through first frost in September, is the best time for harvesting black trumpets.

On my woodlot, black trumpets prefer an old, little-used tote road, or wood-hauling road. Here, the mushrooms have ample shade in summer, little competition from weeds and loose, woodland loam.

When first discovered, this spot amazed me. Dense carpets of black trumpets covered the ground. But at first, I only saw a small group of mushrooms. Kneeling down and scanning the area, hundreds more of these black, brown and gray mushrooms became immediately apparent.

Anyone who has ever sought snowshoe hares in winter, on the snow, will instantly understand my comparison. First, the hare's eye stands out, black, liquid and twinkling. Then, after seeing the eye, the rest of the hare's near-white—hares are slightly off-white, nature's way of giving them a break but not a wholly perfect advantage—body quickly takes form. It's the same with black trumpet mushrooms. So when you find a small group of black trumpets, just keep looking. Odds are that many more will soon become apparent.

Like chanterelles, black trumpets grow in dappled shade of mixed-growth wood-lands. The trumpet-shape of the mushroom perfectly fits the common name.

Black trumpets and chanterelles often appear at the same time and in the same general area.

While picking black trumpets by pulling the fungi up by the roots won't hurt future crops, it does make for harder cleaning later, since dirt and woodland debris sticks to the roots. I prefer to pinch the stem at ground level, leaving the roots in place. This makes for a remarkably clean mushroom.

Given good picking, it takes very little time to fill a large basket with black trumpets. Then it's back home, where the mushrooms are spread out on a table and each individual one picked up by hand and placed in a clean container. These are among the easiest mushrooms to clean, given that you follow my suggestion regarding leaving the roots in place.

To cook black trumpets, melt butter—clarified butter works well too, since it won't scorch—in a frying pan and sprinkle in the mushrooms. No need to break the trumpets up, unless you have extremely large specimens. Stir as they cook and in only a short time, the butter will darken and turn into a near-black ambrosia. It amazes me that these seemingly-dry mushrooms can produce so much liquid. But they do and that's a good thing, because the liquid makes a kind of thin, mushroom gravy.

My favorite way of serving black trumpets is to drain and reserve the juice with the trumpets on one side of a dinner plate and a good scoop of Jasmine rice, or your favorite rice—wild rice works well too—drizzle the mushroom liquid over the rice. When complemented with orache from the seashore or perhaps a late picking of lamb's quarters from the garden, this meal represents the ultimate in fine dining. And it's all available free, from nature.

Black trumpets exhibit their gills as little ridges running down the outside of the horn. The stem, if we can call it that, is really nothing more than the small end of the horn, or trumpet. Black trumpets grow to two or three inches high and between two and four inches in diameter. The horn, or body of the trumpet, is very thin and to my mind, resembles a fine, flexible form of parchment. As mentioned earlier, trumpets come in shades of near-black, gray and a light brown.

Finally, black trumpets lend themselves to freezing. Just prepare as if you were going to serve them at table, but instead, place trumpets and accompanying liquid in a sealed container. I like to save those thick, plastic containers that crabmeat often comes in. These are reusable and work very well for keeping trumpets and other mushrooms safe and like fresh in the freezer.

Note that some years see extraordinarily huge crops of black trumpets and other years, these interesting and delicious mushrooms are scarce and hard to find. But the lean years only serve to tell us how valuable these little woodland morsels truly are.

Coral Mushroom

This ubiquitous late summer mushroom grows in mixed growth woodlands throughout Maine. It is the most common of its type and probably for that reason the most widely used and most easily recognized. One venerable mushroom book refers to this mushroom as, "Ashy Coral Fungus." And that description seems apt, since it has an ashen, gray color.

Other coral-type mushrooms of the species, *Clavaria*, grow in Maine too, but for purposes of keeping mushroom hunting safe and simple, I suggest that beginners stick to the gray variety, at least initially.

These mushrooms grow singly, on the ground, and are prime in early September in Mid-coast Maine. The season for these and other mushrooms comes a bit earlier in northern and western sections and arrives later in southern areas.

In the case of coral mushrooms, the common name really tells the story, since coral fungus, or coral mushrooms, look almost exactly like a clump of branched ocean coral growing on the forest floor.

Let me recommend that you study the photo shown here and commit it to memory. And then, while hunting mushrooms this fall, when encountering a coral mushroom, you will immediately recognize it. Also, rather than look specifically for coral mushrooms (or any one kind, for that matter), remember that other fine mushrooms are available in late summer in Maine's woodlands and corals are just one of them. Therefore, it will pay to become familiar with all the

The grayish-white coral mushrooms look much like a branched coral. These appear in September and persist well into October.

mushroom photos in this book, since knowing their physical properties ahead of time can pay off in dividends later.

Regarding coral mushrooms and in fact, all wild mushrooms, remember that their appearance, while somewhat predictable, cannot be totally relied upon. Some years, in some areas, a certain type of mushroom will abound. And the next year, scarce a one can be seen. So if your quest for coral mushrooms or others mentioned here does not come to fruition this year, don't despair. Another season is just around the corner.

Getting back to coral mushrooms, make sure to check that the mushroom is in its prime. When these age, insects attack them and for that reason, check carefully for insect infestations, especially at the base of the clump. Select only firm, insect-free coral mushrooms. Discard any that are soft, or have a jelly-like texture.

Older corals can develop a bitter taste, but by following the above advice, you'll avoid that, since you won't bother with older mushrooms.

For cooking, many books recommend using these cut-up in soups and stews. That works fine, but in my mind, ashy coral mushrooms taste just fine when gently sautéed in butter or any good butter substitute. They have a very good flavor all of their own and don't need to be added to anything else to make a perfectly enjoyable mushroom dish.

As always, if you have never eaten ashy coral mushrooms, cook just a small amount first, perhaps half a teaspoon, and try it. If it agrees with you, then the next day you are safe to eat more.

Painted Bolete

Some mushrooms are nondescript, while others are the embodiment of natural beauty. Painted bolete mushrooms fall into the latter category.

Painted boletes, *Boletinus pictus*, have scaly, or fuzzy caps and stalks. The "painted" part of their common name alludes to the showy red color of both cap and stalk.

As a bolete, the bottom of the cap has something like pores, or cells, rather than the gills typical of cap-style mushrooms. On painted boletes, these are yellow, contrasting nicely with the rest of the mushroom. The pores, or more properly, "tubes," being inedible, are easily rubbed off with the fingers before preparing for the table.

Boletes encompass a large family of mushrooms and painted bolete is just one of many. But it is surely one of the most striking.

Painted Bolete (clockwise from upper left) caps, stem and cap from above,

Painted boletes grow singly, usually quite far from one another, in woodland loam. However, even a small space can hold many painted boletes. My mixed-growth woodlot hosts painted boletes, and these grow on a disused tote road once used for hauling wood. But no matter where you find painted boletes, you are sure to find white pine trees. Painted boletes always grow in the vicinity of white pines.

After harvesting painted boletes and taking them home, the first step toward getting them table-ready is to remove the bottom layer of tubes. This sponge-like section easily pulls away from the cap. Think of it like peeling a hard-boiled egg. After removing and discarding the shell, the egg is safe for eating.

After removing and discarding the tubes, cut the mushroom up into bite-sized pieces and sauté. Painted boletes, being fairly large and quite dense, give us a good quantity of flesh from only a few mushrooms. And unlike shaggy manes, these handsome mushrooms keep well in the refrigerator. They don't last long in my fridge, though, because they get eaten so quickly.

Their striking physical appearance allows us to spot painted boletes from a great distance. These are delicious mushrooms and here's hoping that you can add painted boletes to your list of edible mushrooms.

Hen Of The Woods

Hen of the woods, *Grifola frondosa*, usually appear at the same place, around the same time, each year. They are, in effect, "perennial" in that regard. A closely-related mushroom, *G. umbellata*, resembles hen of the woods. It, too, is a fine, safe mushroom and it appears at the same time, on the same habitat.

The common name, hen of the woods, never made much sense to me. But one day, while trout fishing a small stream lined by mighty oaks, I saw in the distance something that looked like a Rhode Island red hen. Of course it was *G. frondosa*, hen of the woods.

This specimen, well over a foot in diameter, was at its prime. All thoughts of trout forgotten, I marked the location and climbed the steep bank leading to the road, where my car was parked. Opening the trunk, I grabbed two large canvas shopping bags. Back at the stream, my real work began.

The mushroom grew on an exposed root of a red oak tree, so picking it was no problem. Hen of the woods mushroom consists of many loosely joined caps. If the thing were white rather than brown, it might more closely resemble a piece of coral rather than a hen.

Anyway, when dealing with a mushroom of this size and weight, it is nec-essary to cut the thing in manageable-sized pieces. This I did and still, after stuffing both bags to bulging, enough mushroom remained so that I filled both pockets on my jacket as well as pants pockets. The long uphill hike back to my

Hen of the woods resembles a brown hen with her feathers ruffled.

car was difficult, but I didn't care. I had stumbled upon one of my all-time favorite mushrooms and it was at the peak of perfection.

My first stop was to the home of some friends who often shared their wild mushrooms with me, so it was time to reply in-kind. After that, back home in my kitchen, I laid the largest remaining piece of mushroom on my kitchen table and took a few photographs. Even at little more than half its original size, my hen of the woods was impressive.

Cleaning any mushroom involves some special care. Usually, when picking wild mushrooms, bits of leaf litter, sticks and other debris from the forest floor adhere to the mushroom. In the case of hen of the woods, the valleys and depressions between the caps often hold bits of bark and even small twigs. But don't be tempted to try and wash the foreign matter away.

As with the brown, papery parchment on ostrich fern fiddleheads, washing in water only makes the unwanted material stick to the plant all the more. So cleaning dry is the only solution. I use my jackknife to flick away the debris. If that means cutting away a portion of mushroom, so be it.

So exercise care when picking, and if your mushrooms have any foreign matter on them when you get back home, remove it with a knife or even a small brush. A spare toothbrush works well for this chore.

Now it remained for me to further process my find. This involved placing the mushroom on a cutting board and, with a butcher knife, cutting it into small, bite-sized bits. It took a long time, too, but eventually I managed to fill a large food-storage bag with cut-up mushroom for fresh use and also had a considerable amount left for freezing.

Hen of the woods freezes well and even one year later, if properly cared for, retains the texture and taste of a fresh-picked mushroom. Here's how to prepare your mushroom for the freezer.

After cutting to small pieces, put some oil (margarine works, too, but I prefer oil) in a frying pan and turn heat up to medium. A large mushroom such as hen of the woods is best prepared in a correspondingly-large frying pan.

When the oil has heated, introduce the cut-up mushrooms and stir continually. Cook for no less than three minutes. It won't hurt to cook longer, either, as long as you keep stirring. You may need to add more oil as the mushroom cooks, since it absorbs lots of oil in the process.

After cooking, turn the mushroom and the oil into a large glass bowl and allow to cool by placing the bowl in the refrigerator. When you can safely handle the mushroom, pack it, along with the cooking oil remains, in the sandwich bags mentioned in my section on putting up food for the freezer. Fold the top of the bag and squeeze out all air so that the oil begins to ooze out the side. Then place this in a larger freezer bag. My hen of the woods filled so many sandwich bags that they easily filled a gallon freezer bag, with some left over.

Place the now-full freezer bags in the freezer and your mushroom is put up, safe and fresh for when you need it. Hen of the woods, whether fresh or frozen, is considered choice by mushroom devotees.

Chicken Of The Woods

Oh-oh. We just spoke of hen of the woods and now we have a mushroom called "chicken of the woods?" It's another case of those pesky, common names throwing a spanner in the works. This fine, choice mushroom does not resemble a chicken in any way and it certainly does not taste like chicken, either. Another common name does a better job of describing, *Laetiporus sulphureus*, or sulphur shelf mushroom. The mushroom, indeed, grows on hardwood trees in the manner of lots of little shelves. And the edges are a light yellow, just like sulphur.

Chicken of the woods grows on dead, dying, or otherwise compromised hardwood trees. I find it primarily on black cherry and white ash. It sometimes appears on stumps of softwood trees, too, but only infrequently.

Each "shelf," and there can be many dozens of them on one tree, ranges from several inches in width up to foot. The general shape is that of a somewhat cupped fan. Also, the shelves are waxy-feeling on top and rough on bottom, on account of the many small pores. The bottom is yellow and the top orange.

While these mushrooms can occur singly, they usually appear grown together at the base and stacked up, one upon another. A tree with a large blush of these mushrooms is a striking sight, plainly visible from afar. In fact, one of my bigger finds occurred as I was driving down the highway at fifty miles per hour.

At the bottom of a hill, in a little ravine, I thought I detected something orange in my peripheral vision. So I slowed down, backed up and parked off the side of the road. Walking back, I soon saw what I had hoped awaited me, a cherry tree, the top long gone and the standing trunk absolutely loaded with chicken of the woods mushrooms.

Again, I not only had canvas bags but also a large brown-ash collecting basket, conveniently stashed in my trunk. I filled all the bags as well as my basket with the tenderest of the shelf mushrooms. Some of them were a bit old, which made them too tough for eating.

Shades of the time I found the hen of the woods, I next drove to the nearest town, where some mushroom-loving friends lived and gave them a good supply of chicken of the woods. They had never tried these particular mushrooms, but they trusted me enough to accept my offer. Later, they told me that they thoroughly enjoyed the mushrooms.

While the entire hen of the woods mushroom is edible, only certain parts of chicken of the woods makes for good eating. Usually, the base is too woody and tough to be of any value, so it is the edges that we choose as food. These should be somewhat soft and fairly flexible.

Mushroom hunters rate chicken of the woods, a shelf-type mushroom, as choice.

Prepare these the same way as hen of the woods. They freeze equally well, too, so if you find chicken of the woods and decide that you like it, be sure to freeze some for winter's use.

Oddly enough, these fine mushrooms don't always show up on the same tree every year. But, usually, another tree in the same area will host a crop of chicken of the woods mushrooms. Make sure to check the recipe section here for a fine wild-mushroom omelette recipe.

Puffballs

Puffball mushrooms, *Calvatica* species, come in several sizes, from the tiny, skull-shaped puffball, *C. craniformis*, that grows on dead trees and stumps, to the gem-studded puffball, *C. perlatum*, of gravel banks and decaying logs and the giant puffballs, *C. gigantea*, that erupt overnight along roadsides and on lawns and pastures.

These are the mushrooms that, when fully mature, become filled with dark spores. Stepping on a mature puffball causes great clouds of spores to puff out, thus the common name. But at this point, the mushroom is no longer edible. For that reason, we must choose only ripe, young puffballs that are pure white inside.

Puffballs are pretty much closed, except that the gem-studded variety has a small orifice on its end, a sort of "chimney" for the escaping spores. A prime

Tom holds giant puffballs to demonstrate their great size.

Puffballs are among the most abundant of the choice mushrooms and the easiest to identify.

puffball should feel firm, but not soft. Solid all the way through, puffballs are quite dense. Being all or almost entirely enclosed, puffballs lack gills so typical of cap-type mushrooms. Puffballs lack a true stem, except the lower portion of gem-studded puffballs exhibit the rudimentary shape of a stem.

Young, prime puffballs have white flesh. As the mushroom ages, the flesh turns to yellow, at which point it becomes very bitter. But when the flesh is pure white, with the texture of a block of hard cheese, it is fine.

When picking puffballs, it is important not to confuse the smaller varieties with a young, *Amanita*, a very toxic mushroom. In order to confirm that your mushroom is a puffball, just cut it in half, longitudinally, and if the flesh is pure and clean, with no outline of a small, cap-style mushroom, it is safe.

It doesn't take long to recognize puffballs and, once you acquire this ability, you will be able to spot them along the road while driving and on dead trees and stumps while walking in the woods.

Depending upon rainfall, or lack thereof, puffballs start appearing sometime in late July and continue through September. I have found cup-shaped puffballs in October while bird hunting. In fact, one morning of hard hunting failed to produce one partridge or woodcock, but I took consolation in finding a large puffball, more than enough for my supper that night.

Preparing puffballs, especially smaller ones, is easy. Just rub off any clinging debris and cut them in half. Larger ones need further processing and giant puffballs should be sliced, like tomatoes.

After cutting, I like to douse my puffball pieces with flour and fry in butter to a golden brown.

Puffballs, too, freeze well. I seldom freeze them, though, since they are so delicious that I can't seem to save out enough for freezing. That says something about how well I like puffball mushrooms.

Chaga

Most everyone who spends time outdoors has seen chaga, but only a small percentage recognize it for what it is.

Chaga, *Inonotus obliquus*, no more resembles a mushroom than a rowboat resembles the Queen Mary. And that's the reason for its being hidden in plain sight for so many of us.

Until recent years, I was unaware of what that charred-looking substance growing on white and yellow birch trees was. It always seemed to me that the blackened, crumbly matter was evidence of a past fire. That was not even close.

Then several years ago people began asking me if I was familiar with Chaga. I wasn't, but that oversight was soon corrected. And now it seems as though ev-

Chaga has an appearance of burnt bark.

erywhere my path leads into the woods, there I find chaga. Chaga isn't rare or uncommon, and for those who swear by its curative properties, that's a good thing.

The best way to recognize chaga, other than having someone who is familiar with it show you, is to study photos. After that, it's time to go for a walk in some mixed-growth woodlands to look for the real thing. But remember that unlike other mushrooms, chaga has no specific or well-defined shape. The chaga in the photos shown here has a cylindrical habit, but that was purely a chance form.

So instead of looking for any specific mushroom shape, instead look for something that quite closely resembles the "clinkers" found along railroad tracks, leftovers from the age of steam. Chaga does have some identifiable traits, though. It is generally black (that "burned" look) on the outside and yellowish-brown on the inside. And though hard and dense, chaga is crumbly.

Some foragers suggest using a hammer and chisel to remove chaga from the host tree. I've found that a small hatchet works just fine. Also, when chiseling or chopping a hunk of chaga from a tree, don't worry about getting it all, since the remaining chaga will regenerate and will be ready for harvest several years down the road.

Note that the main reason for consuming chaga is because of its reputed health benefits. People the world over have used chaga medicinally for thousands of years and reports of its benefits are legion. This ugly-looking fungus supposedly cures most known diseases, enhances the immune system and extends people's lifespan. My take is that if only some of these much-vaunted traits are legitimate, it would be worth taking chaga on a regular basis. Besides that, it has no known harmful effects, and when made into a tea, chaga has a distinct maple syrup taste.

Once acquiring some chaga, the next step is figuring out how to use it. Some experts make an alcohol-based chaga extract. The steps involved seem too ambitious for my taste. Since chaga also works when made into a tea, that suits me fine.

My method of rendering chaga into something suitable for making a tea is to take a small hammer and break off perhaps a walnut-sized bit and then grind it down with a kitchen grater. Other folks use a blender or food processor to reduce the chaga to an even finer state, and that's okay. But the stuff I get by the use of my kitchen grader works well, so the extra step of using an electric device isn't really necessary.

To make chaga tea, I place a half-teaspoon of ground mushroom in a teacup and then add boiling water. The amount of chaga can vary according to taste. There is no right or wrong.

Despite claims of chaga being entirely safe, don't take it before consulting with a physician. This warning holds doubly true for those taking prescription medications. Chaga contains so many components that a slight possibility exists that it may cause an undesirable interaction. The chance of that is slight but better safe than sorry.

Finally, authorities suggest that chaga is at its best after a prolonged period in temperatures less than 50 degrees. For that reason, I wait until late fall and even into the winter before harvesting chaga. And when back home, my chaga goes directly into the freezer, where it keeps almost indefinitely.

One final note regarding harvesting chaga. It has become the basis of a new health food craze, and for that reason, health food stores and co-ops eagerly buy chaga from commercial foragers. This selling of wild plants goes against my grain. After all, the reason for this book is to educate people so they can go out and harvest their own useful wild plants, rather than having to purchase them.

Besides that, commercial harvesters often disrespect landowners and harvest without permission. Also, many landowners are aware of chaga and so are displeased, to put it mildly, when a commercial harvester takes all their chaga and leaves nothing for them.

Only a few years ago it was possible to spot chaga while driving along rural roads. But the roadside chaga has gone the way of the dodo bird. And commercial harvesting is mostly to blame.

So only harvest chaga from your own land or from the land where you have permission to forage. That way we will preserve our foraging heritage for years to come.

Winter

Winter, a cold, lifeless season of long, dark days when the wild plants we love so much seem terribly distant. But beneath the snow and ice the plants persist, some in the form of seeds that will germinate when spring sunshine thaws the frozen ground and others as perennial roots, tubers and just plain cold-hardy plants.

So we relax, knowing that come spring, the growing season will return, as it always does. In the meantime, while we wait, we can snub the elements by going "freezer foraging," planning luscious meals centering on our favorite wild edible plants, the ones we so carefully packaged and frozen.

Recipes

In the chapters on different seasonal plants, I have included basic preparation methods. These are by no means the only ways to prepare the wild plants. Any recipe or method given here is meant to be flexible. So, modify my suggestions, bend them to your own taste. Try what appeals to you and by all means, don't hesitate to experiment. Recipes, at least those I offer, are never meant to be static, unchanging. Rather, they are only basic guidelines.

Also, it's always fun to substitute wild plants for cultivated vegetables in standard recipes. Casseroles, soups, quiches, omelets and other dishes really shine when you include wild edible plants.

This last chapter details some of my favorite wild plant recipes. Perhaps you will try some of them. If you do, I sincerely hope you enjoy them. Best wishes for a lifetime of enjoyment from Maine's useful, wild plants.

Pickled Pickerel

This recipe uses the leaves of northern bay as a flavoring for pickled fish. Chain pickerel, abundant in Maine, lend themselves to pickling. The finished product resembles the pickled herring seen in seafood coolers. If you like pickled herring, you will probably love pickerel. Here is the recipe.

Collect the following:
> 6 skinless fillets from 14- to 16-inch pickerel
> 2 small-to-medium onions sliced very thin
> 1 cup white vinegar
> ½ cup water
> 2 ounces sugar
> 1 teaspoon allspice
> ¼ teaspoon salt
> ¼ teaspoon ground pepper
> fresh or dried leaves of northern bay
> salt

Next, rinse and drain fillets and coat heavily with salt on both sides. Place in a bowl, cover and let stand in refrigerator for twenty-four hours. Rinse well, pat dry and cut into bite-sized pieces. Pack these into eight-ounce jelly or canning jars. Wide-mouth jars are best. Use alternating layers of fish and onion. Finally, tuck bay leaves down alongside contents. Use as many bay leaves as you can squeeze in.

Mix vinegar, water, sugar, allspice, salt and pepper in a glass measuring cup and stir until sugar dissolves. Slowly pour solution into jars, tapping as you go in order to dislodge trapped air bubbles. Fill to brim and screw down cap, tightly. Refrigerate. Fish is ready in three days, although waiting longer allows a stronger flavor to develop. Keeps about three weeks.

While I haven't tried it, alewives would no doubt make a good substitute for pickerel using this recipe. They are in the same family as herring, as mentioned earlier, are pickled on a commercial basis.

Blue Mussels

The next recipe uses northern bay leaves to flavor blue mussels. When cooking these, I use no water but instead rely upon the liquid within the shellfish for cooking. The resulting broth is true nectar, heady and aromatic. Here is my basic recipe.

Fill a large saucepan about half full with fresh mussels. To this, add three or four leaves of northern bay. Slice half of one small white onion very thin and sprinkle this on top of the shellfish. Cover and turn up heat to high. When the top jiggles, remove it and place back on so that it is tilted in order to allow steam to escape. Turn heat down just enough so that the water does not boil over. Cook for at least five minutes, more or less according to the size of saucepan and also the shellfish.

When all shells are open, remove from heat, drain and reserve liquid. Serve piping hot, with teacups of hot broth for dipping.

If any mussels remain from this meal, remove meats from the shells and place in a glass jar. Add two northern bay leaves and cover with white vinegar. Refrigerate. Ready in about twenty-four hours.

Also, if you find a number of steamed clams left over after a summertime picnic, just remove the meats and treat as shown above for blue mussels.

Stovies

Scotland has always embraced edible wild plants and the following two suggestions are variations of traditional Scottish recipes.

Gather together:
   1 pound thickly sliced groundnuts
   2 large onions, sliced
   2 ounces pan or roasting rack drippings from roast beef, pork or ham
   salt
   pepper
Use an iron saucepan or Dutch oven, one with a tight-fitting lid. Add drippings and turn heat on high, until it begins to smoke. Turn down to medium and add onions and groundnuts and sprinkle with sea salt and ground black pepper. Cover and allow to simmer for 45 minutes. Do not lift lid. When ready, stir contents with a heavy wooden spoon.

   This recipe works with Jerusalem artichokes, too, but the cooking time is longer. The original Scottish recipe called for potatoes.

Nettle Soup

This recipe dates back to a time when Scotland's beloved bard, Robert Burns was writing his famous verses. Nettles are an ancient food of the Highlanders and no one really knows how far the practice of eating wild nettles dates back.

Gather together:
   1 quart chicken stock
   8 large handfuls of chopped nettle leaves
   1 medium-sized onion
   1 ounce flour
   1 ounce butter
   salt and pepper
Wash and chop the nettles and chop the onion to small bits. In a large saucepan, add the butter and nettle tops, cooking them until fork-tender. Add the flour, stock and salt and pepper to taste. Bring to a boil and simmer for five minutes. Add a dash of heavy cream before serving, if desired.

Knotweed Chutney

This product is a staple in my house. When preparing it, my kitchen fills with a spicy, pungent aroma.

Gather together:

2 pounds Japanese knotweed stem tips, cut into inch-long sections. Make sure to use either tender young shoots, or if, using larger stems, peel them, discarding any stringy material.

2 lemons, grate the peels and retain the pulp

2 cloves crushed garlic

1- to 2-inch ginger root, peeled

3 cups honey

1 1/2 cups cider vinegar

2 teaspoons salt

Place all ingredients in a large saucepan. Turn heat to high. Bring to a boil, while stirring constantly. Continue boiling and stirring (this may take some time. If you have a helper, it might be good to take turns stirring) until mixture thickens. Then, remove the ginger root and pour into sterilized 8-ounce canning jars. Seal with new tops and screw lids down tightly. The heat from the mixture suffices to seal the top. Allow to sit on a dark shelf for six weeks before using. A lot of work, but well worth it. Makes 7 eight-ounce jars.

Garlic Knotweed

8 oz tender shoots of Japanese knotweed.

1-2 tbsp butter

2 minced garlic cloves

1 teaspoon coarse salt (or to taste)

Melt butter in a 10- to 12-inch frying pan over medium heat. Add garlic and cook for 30 seconds. Add knotweed shoots and continue to stir until butter begins to caramelize. Cover, reduce to low heat and simmer for 10-15 minutes or until knotweed shoots are tinder. Season with salt and serve.

Fiddlehead and Cheese Sauce Casserole

Ostrich fern fiddleheads excel in so many different recipes. This and those following are some of my favorite, fiddlehead recipes.
Gather together:
2 pints cooked and drained fiddleheads
one quart Alfredo sauce
breadcrumbs
Line the bottom of a casserole dish with fiddleheads and then drizzle with Alfredo sauce. Add another layer of fiddleheads and cover them with sauce. Continue alternating the two until the fiddleheads are used up and the top layer is covered with Alfredo sauce. Sprinkle unseasoned breadcrumbs over the sauce and bake at 325° for about 40 minutes, or until the crumbs begin to turn brown. Serve as is or over egg noodles. This recipe presents a fine way to use those frozen fiddleheads in winter.

Fiddlehead Salad

Cook and drain fiddleheads. This also works for frozen fiddleheads. Place in a bowl, cover and refrigerate. Prior to serving, sprinkle with fresh-ground black pepper and pour on Italian salad dressing. Or, use homemade oil-and-vinegar as a substitute. Before serving, sprinkle lightly with Parmesan cheese.

Canned Fiddleheads

I preserve fiddleheads through canning each year and am pleased to open them in February, just when I'm yearning for spring and fresh plants on my menu. Can them following the directions with your canning device. Now you can even can in the electric cookers that are a hybrid of a pressure cooker, slow cooker or cooking pot. Canned fiddleheads can be used in any recipe where you would use fresh. My friend and publisher, Nancy Randolph adds them to salads. Just rinse, dry and top off any salad for a taste of spring.

Nancy's Fiddleheads

This recipe is a wonderful way to use your frozen fiddleheads that you have gathered and frozen during early spring. Courtesy of Just Write Books publisher, Nancy Randolph. By the way, this works well with either fresh or frozen fiddleheads.

Assemble:

4 cups lightly cooked fiddleheads
1/3 cup slivered almonds
3 tbsp butter
salt & pepper (to taste)

Set 2" water to boil in medium saucepan.

Add frozen fiddleheads and return to boil. Stir with fork until fiddleheads separate. Remove from water and drain immediately and set aside.

Heat butter in wok or large frying pan. Add almonds and stir until almonds begin to brown. Add fiddleheads and stir for 2 to 4 minutes.

Serve immediately. Drizzle lemon juice or add extra butter at table as desired.

Penny's Sauteed Fiddleheads

Gather together:

1 pound cleaned fiddleheads
2 garlic cloves, finely minced
¼ cup butter, oil or margarine
2 teaspoons finely chopped, fresh parsley
salt and black pepper to taste

Heat half of the butter or oil in pan over medium heat. Add fiddleheads and turn heat to medium-high. Fiddleheads should sizzle, but don't allow to burn or scorch. Toss and stir for 5 minutes. Add remaining butter or oil, garlic and parsley. Continue cooking 1 minute longer or until fiddleheads are tender and crisp, but do not overcook. Season to taste.

Wilted Dandelion Salad

This recipe is courtesy of my publisher. She remembers as a child having this with bacon fat. Since she no longer eats meat, she has adjusted the recipe for vegetarians.

Gather together:

6 oz harvested dandelion greens (cleaned with roots removed)

2 tbsp olive oil

1 onion chopped

1 tbsp maple syrup

2 cloves of minced garlic

Heat oil in a skillet over medium heat.

Add onion and maple syrup; cook, stirring occasionally, until onion is golden and has caramelized, about 15 minutes.

Add garlic; cook, stirring occasionally, 2 minutes.

Add dandelion greens, and toss to combine. Cook until greens have just wilted, about 1 minute.

NOTE: If you want to make this with bacon, cook three slices of bacon according to your favorite method. With a slotted spoon remove the bacon and substitute the bacon grease for olive oil. Save the bacon to crumble and add to the top of the greens when plating.

India-style Dandelion

Assemble ingredients for sauce:
¼ cup canola oil
1 medium onion chopped
2 cloves garlic minced
1 inch ginger root peeled and minced
1 tbsp red pepper flakes (adjust to taste)
2 tsp curry powder or garam masala
½ tsp chili powder
large pinch sugar
salt & pepper to taste
2 cups chopped red tomato or canned tomatoes (drained)
½ cup cream, half & half or coconut milk
½ cup fresh cilantro leaves (1/8 c. dried)
1 tsp cumin seed
1 tsp mustard seed

Saute onion, garlic and ginger root in the canola oil until the onions are translucent. Add red pepper flakes, curry powder or *garam masala*, chili powder, sugar, salt and pepper (to taste). Stir in the spices and add the tomatoes and cook for 10-12 minutes. Then add the cream or milk, cilantro, cumin and mustard seeds. Cook at medium for five minutes. Remove from heat and set aside.

Preheat oven to 400° and oil a 2-quart casserole dish.
Assemble ingredients for main recipe:
Sauce (recipe above)
Use 4 cups of dandelions cooked and chopped.
2 cups garbanzo beans (chickpeas)
1 ½ cup cubed Indian cottage or very mild cheese.

Spread sauce on bottom of dish. Then add a layer of dandelions then a layer of beans. Spread the cheese cubes around the top of the dish, slightly press cubes into ingredients below.

Bake for 20 minutes or until cheese and beans have browned.

Simple Woods Scramble

Gather ingredients:
1-2 tbsp canola oil or mild olive oil
½ cup. mushrooms chopped (hen of the woods or chicken of the woods)
½ cup sliced scallions
½ medium onion minced
5 eggs beaten (whole or whites only or combination of whites and yolks)
¼ cup Swiss cheese shredded
salt and pepper to taste
Heat oil then add mushrooms, scallions and onions. Cook at medium-high heat until mushrooms release their liquid. Turn heat down to medium then add eggs stirring slowly but constantly until eggs are nearly set. Add cheese. Continue to stir and cook for another minute. Salt and pepper to taste. Serve immediately.

Chanterelles

Chanterelles add color and taste to any dish. My favorite, though, consists of chopped chanterelles fried in butter and used as a topping on a steak. Cook the mushrooms until slightly brown, but not yet crisp. Then just spoon over a steak fresh from the grill. Sometimes, chanterelles work best as a side dish. A small serving of chopped, fried chanterelles complements an otherwise drab platter.

Coral Mushrooms

The commonly accepted method of preparing coral mushrooms calls for chopping them into bits with a knife or slaw cutter and adding them to home-made soups. That works fine, of course. But these tasty mushrooms shine in their own rite and as such, work well when fried or sautéed and served as a side, along with squash or carrots.

Blueberries

Blueberries fresh from the bush, blueberries in pies, yogurt, muffins and pancakes and in fruit salads. Blueberries seem the ultimate berry for baking. But here is a recipe that requires only frozen blueberries and some maple syrup. No cooking needed.

Freeze cleaned, dried berries. When needed, remove desired amount from freezer and place in a small dessert bowl. Allow to partially thaw. Check to see that berries still contain some ice crystals and then pour on a tablespoon of real maple syrup. The ice-cold berries will cause the syrup to form a thin, frozen crust on each berry.

Elderberry Fritters

Gather elderberry flower clusters. Check for insects. Next, add enough cooking oil to thoroughly cover the bottom of a cast-iron frying pan or skillet and place on medium heat. These fritters don't require deep-frying, although that certainly is an option.

Next, dip the flower clusters in a pancake batter, either pre-mixed or made-from-scratch. Shake off any clinging, or excess batter and fry as per pancakes. Flip as needed. Both sides should turn golden-brown. The fritters are done when they no longer bounce back when pressed with a fork. Serve with maple syrup or molasses. Or just coat with confectioner's sugar. I also like them with butter, salt and pepper.

Milkweed Blossom Fritters

Gather milkweed blossom clusters. (note instructions on page 59-60)
Assemble ingredients for batter:

½ cup flour (this can be gluten-free garbanzo bean flour)
1 egg
½ cup milk (more or less to make a thin batter)
pinch of cayenne pepper
salt & black pepper to taste
Using a wisk mix flour, egg, milk and spices together until smooth.

Add enough cooking oil to thoroughly cover the bottom of a cast-iron frying pan or skillet and place on medium heat. Just as for elderberry fritters, these do not require deep-frying.

Next, dip the flower clusters in a batter, Shake off any clinging, or excess batter and fry as per pancakes. Flip as needed. Both sides should turn golden-brown. The fritters are done when they no longer bounce back when pressed with a fork. Serve as a side to your main dish of fish, meat or veggie entre.

Add Northern Bay Nutlets to Meat and Seafood

Northern Bay nutlets and leaves share similar properties. Nutlets, though, have a more familiar appearance and those not used to wild foods may find the berries more acceptable.

Try adding a scant handful of Northern Bay nutlets to a boiled corned beef. These will add a slightly different flavor than the standard "flavor packet" of spices usually included with a fresh corned beef.

Also, add six or eight Northern Bay nutlets to a half-pint canning jar when pickling blue mussels. Fill the jar with cooked mussel meats, drop in the nutlets and fill nearly to the brim with white vinegar. Refrigerate immediately and allow to sit for one week before using.

Trout lily

Sometimes simple is best. And in the case of trout lilies, that goes double. These ephemeral treats have a delicate flavor and as such, deserve strict attention during the cooking process. Trout lily leaves work best when briefly simmered in a little water.

Wait until other components of a meal become nearly ready for serving before dropping a large handful of trout lily leaves in about ½ -inch of boiling water. Stir, turn the heat down so the leaves simmer and cook only until the leaves turn a dark green and become limp. Then drain thoroughly and serve immediately.

Salt complements trout lily leaves, but pepper does not. Butter or a splash of olive oil is optional.

Wild Mint

The sprightly zest of our wild, native mint has no peer. Where other mints try, wild mint succeeds. This powerful mint has countless uses, but two outstanding ones are dried, as a sprinkle on lamb chops or lamb burgers and also, as the main ingredient in a cooling, summertime iced tea.

To use the dried mint as a meat flavoring, just place a small amount of the dried product between thumb and forefinger and roll it in order to break it up into a finer granulation. Then sprinkle lightly on chops or burgers prior to grilling or broiling.

Use only a little at first, since a little goes a long way. Increase amounts according to taste.

Mint tea, or more succinctly put, a tea made of wild mint, quenches thirst and enlivens the taste buds. Place about ½ cup of dried mint in a pitcher. Fill with boiling water and allow to steep. Then strain into another pitcher and place in the refrigerator. Serve as is, without sugar or lemon. And prepare for a taste explosion.

Elderberry Cordial

4 quarts of elderberries
1 quarts cold water
8 cups sugar
½ tablespoon each, whole allspice, cloves and cinnamon stick
1 quart whisky or brandy

Tie spices in a cheesecloth bag. Pick over and wash berries. Place in a large stainless steel kettle, cover with water, let boil until thoroughly soft; then strain well. Measure, and to each quart of juice add 2 cups sugar. Add spice bag and boil 20 minutes, or until thicken. Let cool and measure again. to each quart of syrup, ad 1 pint of whisky. Bottle and cork tightly. (Using an old-fashioned beer bottle with hinged lid works well.)

From *The Settlement Cookbook*, 1948.

Elderberry Jelly

Take equal parts of elderberries and apples. Cover with water and boil. Mash strain. To 1 cup juice, take 1 cup sugar. Boil juice, skim, add sugar heated. Boil until it jells.

Wash jars and lids with soapy water, dry bands, and set aside. Place jars in a large pot and cover with water. Bring to a simmer. Put lids in a separate pot of hot water. Leave jars and lids in water until ready to fill. Lift jars out of hot water one at a time, draining water.

Ladle hot jelly into hot jars using a funnel, leaving 1/2-inch headspace. Slide a nonmetallic spatula or chopstick between jam and jar to release trapped air bubbles.

Wipe rim and threads of jar with a clean, damp cloth. Remove lid from hot water. Place lid on jar. Screw band down evenly and firmly (do not twist tight.).

Place in wire basket if available otherwise lower into water with canning tongs. Put lid on pot. Bring water to a boil. Start keeping time after water comes to a rolling boil. Process 1/2 pints 10 minutes at a gentle but steady boil.

Turn off heat and remove canner lid. Let canner cool 5 minutes, then remove jars and set them to cool for 12-24 hours on a dry towel or rack. Do not retighten bands.

From *The Settlement Cookbook*, 1948.

Dandelion Wine

1 gallon dandelion flowers
1 gallon boiling water
6 cups sugar
3 oranges, cut in small pieces
3 lemons, cut in small pieces
1 oz. yeast

Pick dandelion flowers early in the morning, taking care not to have a particle of the bitter stem attached. Place in large glass, stainless steel or pottery container. Pour boiling water over the flowers and let stand 3 days. Strain and ad the rest of the ingredients; let stand to ferment 3 weeks. Strain and bottle.

From The Settlement Cookbook, 1948.

Staghorn Sumac "Pink Lemonade"

1 quart of cold water
¼ - ½ cup of Sumac berries

Steep the sumac berries in the cold water for one hour. Strain the steeped "pink lemonade" and pour into an ice-filled glass. May be sweetened with honey, sugar or maple syrup. May also be used as is in any recipe calling for lemon juice.

Resources for Foragers

Coon, Nelson. *Using Plants for Healing*, Rodale Press, Emmaus, Pennsylvania, 1979.

Henderson, Peter. *Henderson's Handbook of Plants and General Horticulture.* Peter Henderson and Company: New York, 1904.

National Audubon Society. *Pocket Guide to Familiar Mushrooms*, National Audobon Society, Knopf: New York, NY, 1990.

Pratt, Anne. *The Flowering Plants of Great Britain*. Frederick Warne, London [ca 1870]

Seymour, Tom. *Foraging New England*, Tom Seymour. Globe Pequot Press: Guilford, CT, 2002.

www.naturaldatabase.com

Books by Tom Seymour

Wild Plants of Maine, Third Edition, Just Write Books (JWB), 2018

Nuts And Berries Of New England, Globe Pequot Press (GPP), 2013

Foraging New England, GPP, 2002, 2013

Maine Wildlife, Up-Close and Personal Encounters of a Maine Naturalist, The Maine Sportsman, 2005

Birding Maine, GPP, 2008

Off The Beaten Path Maine, GPP, 2011

Fishing Maine, GPP, 1996, 2007

Hiking Maine, GPP, 1995, 2002

Tom Seymour's Maine: A Maine Anthology, iUniverse Press, 2003

Hidden World Revealed: Musings of a Maine Naturalist, (JWB), 2008

Wild Plants of Maine, JWB, 2010

Tom Seymour's Forager's Notebook, JWB, 2011

Index

Alliaria petiolate   38-40

Amaranthus retroflexus   99-100

Amelanchier laevis   89-91

Anaphalis margaritacea   78-79

Apios Americana   42-44

Aralia nudicaulis   45-46

Armoracia rusticana   50-51

Arrowhead (*Sagittaria latifolia*)   87-88

Asclepias syriaca   57-60

Aster macrophyllus   30-31

Atriplex patula   115-117

Barbarea vulgaris   36-38

basket   3

Beach Pea (*Lathyrus japonicus*)   109-111

Beaked Hazelnuts (*Corylus cornuta*)   85-86

Beechnut (*Fagus grandifolia*)   133-136

Black Trumpets (*Craterellus fallax*)   142-145

blackflies   15

Blue Mussels (*Mytilus edulis*)   160

Blueberries (*Vaccinium corymbosum*)   84-85, 167

Blunt-Leaved Dock (*Rumex obtusifolius*)   13-15

Boletinus pictus   147-148

Boneset (*Eupatorium perfoliatum*)   126-127

Browne, William   14

Browne's *Britannia's Pastorals*   14

Browne's *Pastorals*   14

Bumblebee weed   67

Cakile edentula   114-115

Calvatica species   152-154

Canada Goldenrod (*Solidago canadensis*)   127-128

Canned Fiddleheads   163

Cantharellus cibarius   140-142, 167

Cattail (*Typha latifolia*)   60-62

Cattail Sprouts   10-11

Chaga (*Inonotus obliquus*)   154-156

Chanterelles (Cantharellus cibarius)   140-142, 167

Chenopodium album   96-98

chewing gum replacement   78

Chicken of the Woods (*Laetiporus sulphureus*)   150-152

Chrysanthemum leucanthemum   76-77

Clavaria   145-146, 167

Clintonia (*Clintonia borealis*)   34-35

Clintonia borealis   34-35

Coltsfoot (*Tussilago farfara*)   12-13

Comfrey (*Symphytum officinale*)   55-57

Common Blue Violet (*Viola papilionacea*)   40-42

Common Milkweed (*Asclepias syriaca*)   57-60

Common Plantain (*Plantago major*) 63-64
Comptonia perigrina 71-73
Coprinus comatus 138-140
Coptis groenlandica 123
Coral Mushroom (*Clavaria*) 145-146, 167
Corylus cornuta 85-86
Craterellus fallax 142-145
Curled Dock (*Rumex crispus*) 20-21
Dame's Rocket (*Hesperis matronalis*) 52-54
Dandelion (*Taraxacum officinale*) 15-17
dandelion digger 3
Dandelion Wine 171
Daucus carota 69-71
Daylilies (*Hemerocallis fulva*) 74-76
DEET 4
Eastern Hemlock (*Tsuga Canadensis*) 131-133
Elderberry (*Sambucus canadensis*) 81-83
Elderberry Cordial 170
Elderberry Fritters 168
Elderberry Jelly 170
Erythronium americanum 27-28, 169
Eupatorium maculatum 100-101, 126-127
Evening Primrose (*Oenothera biennis*) 2, 7-9
Fagus grandifolia 133-136
Fall 123-136
False Solomon's Seal (*Smilacina racemose*) 32-33
Fiddlehead and Cheese recipe 163
Fiddlehead Salad recipe 163

Fiddleheads (Ostrich Fern) (*Matteuccia strathiopteris*) 17-19
freezing 16, 17, 25, 60, 82, 85, 96, 98, 102, 117, 118, 145, 150, 152, 154, 156
Galinsoga (*Galinsoga ciliate*) 91-92
Galinsoga ciliate 91-92
Garlic Knotweed recipe 162
Garlic Mustard (*Alliaria petiolate*) 38-40
Gaultheria procumbens 128-130
Gibbons, Euell 10, 38
Glasswort (*Salicornia virginica*) 112-114
gloves 11, 23, 25, 59, 86
Goldthread (*Coptis groenlandica*) 123
Goosetongue (*Plantago juncoides*) 117-120
Great Depression 1
Green Amaranth (*Amaranthus retroflexus*) 99-100
Grifola frondosa 148-150
Groundnuts (*Apios Americana*) 42-44
Heal-All (*Prunella vulgaris*) 67-68
Hemerocallis fulva 74-76
Hen of the Woods (*Grifola frondosa*) 148-150
Hesperis matronalis 52-54
Hypericum perforatum 107-108
ice chest 4
Impatiens capensis 29-30, 101-102
Indian Cucumber (*Medeola virginiana*) 64-65
India-style Dandelion 166
Inonotus obliquus 154-156

insect repellant 4

Japanese Knotweed (*Polygonum cuspidatum*) 21-23

Jewelweed (*Impatiens capensis*) 29-30, 101-102

Joe-Pye Weed (*Eupatorium maculatum*) 100-101

Knotweed Chutney 162

Lady's Thumb (*Polygonum persicaria*) 93-94

Laetiporus sulphureus 150-152

Lamb's Quarters (*Chenopodium album*) 96-98

Large-Leaved Aster (*Aster macrophyllus*) 30-31

Lathyrus japonicus 109-111

leaf's shape 5

Lepidium campestre 95-96

Maine's Seashore 109-122

Matricaria matricarioides 68-69

Matteuccia strathiopteris 17-19

Medeola virginiana 64-65

medicine (folk) 5, 26, 39, 41, 51, 55, 65, 67, 79, 83, 100, 107, 123, 124, 125, 127

Mentha arvensis 47-50, 169

Milkweed Blossom Fritters 168

Mitchella repens 45

Myrica pensylvanica 119-122

Mytilus edulis 160

Nancy's Fiddlehead recipe 164

naturaldatabase.com 5

Nettle Soup 161

Northern Bay (*Myrica pensylvanica*) 119-122

Northern Bay Nutlets recipe 168

nutlets 55, 73, 77, 121, 122

Oenothera biennis 7-9

Omega vitamins 89

Orache (*Atriplex patula*) 115-117

Orpine (*Sedum purpureum*) 19-20

Oxeye Daisy (*Chrysanthemum leucanthemum*) 76-77

Painted Bolete Mushroom (*Boletinus pictus*) 147-148

Partridgeberry (*Mitchella repens*) 45

Pastinaca sativa 103-104

Pearley Everlasting (*Anaphalis margaritacea*) 78-79

Penny's Sauteed Fiddleheads recipe 164

Peppergrass (*Lepidium campestre*) 95-96

picaridin 4

Pickerelweed (*Pontederia cordata*) 54-55

Pickled Pickerel recipe 159

Pineapple Weed (*Matricaria matricarioides*) 68-69

Pinus strobus 130-132

Plantago juncoides 117-120

Plantago major 63-64

pods 40, 57, 28, 59, 60, 96, 101, 110, 111, 114, 115

Poison ivy remedy 73, 101, 102

Poison ivy 4, 45, 46

Polygonum cuspidatum 21-23

Polygonum persicaria 93-94

Pontederia cordata 54-55

Portulaca oleracea 88-89

potherb 9, 21, 25, 28, 30, 31, 36, 41, 52, 53, 56, 89, 92, 93, 99, 112, 117

poultice 56

Prunella vulgaris 67-68

Puffballs (*Calvatica species*) 152-154

Purple Trillium (*Trillium erectum*) 26-27

Purslane (*Portulaca oleracea*) 88-89

Queen Anne's Lace (*Daucus carota*) 69-71

Recipes 159-171

Rhus typhina 106-107

root crop 7, 50, 53, 56, 64, 65, 66, 70, 75, 100, 101, 104, 123, 124, 125

rubber boots 11

rubber gloves 11

Rumex crispus 20-21

Rumex obtusifolius 13-15

Sagittaria latifolia 87-88

salad 11, 16, 19, 20, 27, 30, 34, 35, 36, 39, 54, 61, 63, 72, 89, 94, 95, 96, 97, 112, 114, 115, 116, 117, 120

Salicornia virginica 112-114

Sambucus canadensis 81-83

Saponaria officinalis 104-106

Sauce Casserole 163

Scutellaria lateriflora 94-95

Sea Blite (*Suaeda maritima*) 111-112

Sea Rocket (*Cakile edentula*) 114-115

Sedum purpureum 19-20

Serviceberry (*Amelanchier laevis*) 89-91

Shaggy Mane Mushroom (*Coprinus comatus*) 138-140

Simple Woods Scramble 167

Skullcap (*Scutellaria lateriflora*) 94-95

Smilacina racemosa 32-33

snuff replacement 78

Soapwort (*Saponaria officinalis*) 104-106

Solidago canadensis 127-128

Spring 7-46

St. Johnswort (*Hypericum perforatum*) 107-108

Staghorn Sumac (*Rhus typhina*) 106-107

Staghorn Sumac "Pink Lemonade" 171

Stinging Nettles (*Urtica dioica*) 23-25

stir-fry recipes 11, 61, 89

Stovies 161

Suaeda maritima 111-112

Summer 47-108

Sweetfern (*Comptonia perigrina*) 71-73

Symphytum officinale 55-57

Tanacetum vulgare 79-81

Tansy (*Tanacetum vulgare*) 79-81

Taraxacum officinale 15-17

tea 46, 47, 49, 50, 66, 69, 70, 72, 73, 83, 95, 100, 102, 108, 126, 127, 129, 130, 132, 133, 156

tools 2

tote bags 4

trail nibble 19, 20, 32, 33, 34, 41, 45, 61, 65, 77, 90, 96, 111, 112, 113, 114, 116, 119, 129

Trillium erectum 26-27

Trout Lily (*Erythronium americanum*) 27-28, 169

Tsuga Canadensis 131-133

Tussilago farfara 12-13

Typha latifolia 60-62

Urtica dioica 23-25

Vaccinium corymbosum 84-85, 167

Valerian (*Valeriana officinalis*) 65-67

Valeriana officinalis 65-67

Viola papilionacea 40-42

Violet syrup 41

vitamin A 20, 27, 38, 39, 89, 130,

vitamin C 20, 27, 37, 38, 39, 41, 89, 130,

waterborne illness 11

White Pine (*Pinus strobus*) 130-132

wild clematis 4

Wild Horseradish (*Armoracia rusticana*) 50-51

Wild Mint (*Mentha arvensis*) 47-50, 169

Wild Mushrooms 137-156

Wild Oats (*Smilacina racemose*) 33

Wild Parsnip (*Pastinaca sativa*) 103-104

Wild Sarsaparilla (*Aralia nudicaulis*) 45-46

Wilted Dandelion Salad 165

Winter 157

Wintercress (*Barbarea vulgaris*) 36-38

Wintergreen (*Gaultheria procumbens*) 128-130

Order Tom's Books

☐ *Forager's Notebook (Undated journal)*

Record your wild plant harvesting in this book—when you forage, what plants you find, where you find them, how you use or prepare your wild plants. You can use one book over and over or purchase one for each new year's use. Your book will become a time capsule of your days of foraging and a memory book for you and your family.

Hardcover, pages 100, Price: $20.00

☐ *Hidden World Revealed: Musings of a Maine Naturalist*

Seymour discusses his interaction with animal neighbors and explores plants and seasonal changes. The narratives of his walks in the woods are instructive about the natural environment and revealing of a human who walks lightly on the earth. A humble man with a fine mind invites us to know our Maine woodlands and rural neighbors.

Softcover, pages 174, Price: $14.95 US

☐ *Wild Plants of Maine: A Useful Guide*

From insect repellent to table fare to a relaxing wintergreen tea, Tom Seymour identifies the source and describes the method of preparing wild plant concoctions or foods. Any person living or visiting in Maine should have this book to ensure the enjoyment of our great Maine outdoors.

Softcover, pages 192, Price: $24.95 US

☐ *Getting Your Big Fish: Trolling in Maine*

Find your big trout in the smaller waters of Maine. Catch trout that are measured in pounds rather than inches. Tom Seymour supplies up-to-date information on tackle and reveals many helpful tricks. Tom has fished these waters for decades.

Softcover, p. 124, Price: $19.95 US

Buy the books above at your local bookstore or purchase them at your favorite online retailer such as amazon.com or www.barnesandnoble.com.

Wild Plant Seminars

Tom Seymour

Phone: (207) 338-9746,
or
Mailing address:
    Tom Seymour
    28 Loggin Road
    Frankfort, Maine 04438
    email: tomgseymour@gmail.com.

    Tom conducts wild plant seminars throughout mid-coast, central and parts of northern Maine for individuals, groups and organizations both public and non-profit. These consist of both narrated digital slide shows with question-and-answer sessions and also, field trips to private and public lands where Tom identifies and explains the uses and properties of local wild plants.

    These field trips begin in spring, usually late April or early May and conclude in September. Times vary, but most trips require from one to two hours. Tom also offers a combination of slide shows and field trips for his seminars.

About Tom Seymour

    An avid writer as well as a naturalist, Seymour writes columns and a multitude of features including his ever-popular "Maine Wildlife" for *The Maine Sportsman Magazine*. *Seymour's other credits include articles in Fur-Fish-Game, Maine Fish and Wildlife, Backpacker Magazine, Northern Woodlands People, Places, Plants and Maine Food & Lifestyle Magazine, among others.* Seymour wrote a long-running, award-winning column "Waldo County Outdoors" for *The Republican Journal (TRJ)*. He writes a garden column for Courier Publications and opinion pieces for TRP. Seymour wrote *Hiking Maine, Fishing Maine, Foraging New England, Birding Maine and Nuts, Berries of New England* and *Mushrooms Maine* for Globe Pequot Press (GPP) and *Wild Plants of Maine: A Useful Guide, Hidden World Revealed: Musings of a Maine Naturalist* and his *Forager's Notebook* for Just Write Books. . He lives in a small cabin in Waldo, Maine.

Milton Keynes UK
Ingram Content Group UK Ltd.
UKHW020948290823
427670UK00010B/63